BEYOND

Other Books by I. A. Richards

The Meaning of Meaning (*with* C. K. Ogden)
1923

Principles of Literary Criticism
1925

Practical Criticism
1929

Coleridge on Imagination
1935

The Philosophy of Rhetoric
1936

Interpretation in Teaching
1938

How to Read a Page
1942

Speculative Instruments
1955

"A Leak in the Universe" (*in* Playbook)
1956

Goodbye Earth and Other Poems
1958

The Screens and Other Poems
1960

Tomorrow Morning, Faustus!
1962

So Much Nearer: Essays Toward a World English
1968

Design for Escape
1968

Internal Colloquies
1971

I. A. Richards

BEYOND

Harcourt Brace Jovanovich

New York and London

Printed in the United States of America

Chapter 6 originally appeared, in somewhat different form,
in the *Michigan Quarterly Review.*

Library of Congress Cataloging in Publication Data

Richards, Ivor Armstrong, 1893–
Beyond.

1. Literature–Philosophy.   2.   Literature–
History and criticism.   I.   Title.
PN49.R47   1974   801'.9   73–18249
ISBN 0–15–111985–6

First edition

B C D E

To

Maxwell E. Foster

most alerting

and restorative of

critics

Disciple: Confucius said: "Water! Ah Water!" What can we learn from that?

Mencius: Consider a pond. The sun beats down. Where is the water? Consider a spring. The water wells out. Never does it cease flowing.

Meta-semantic Markers

(*Specialized Quotation Marks*)

We all recognize—more or less unsystematically—that quotation marks serve varied purposes:

(1) Sometimes they show merely that we are quoting and where our quotation begins and ends.

(2) Sometimes they imply that the word or words within them are in some way open to question and are only to be taken in some special sense with reference to some special definition.

(3) Sometimes they suggest further that what is quoted is nonsense or that there is really no such thing as the thing they profess to name.

(4) Sometimes they suggest that the words are being improperly used. The quotation marks are equivalent to "the so-called."

(5) Sometimes they only indicate that we are talking of the words as distinguished from their meanings. "Is" and "at" are shorter than "above." "Chien" means what "dog" means, and so on.

There are many other uses. This short list will suffice to show how heavily we overwork this too serviceable writing device. Some of these uses accordingly are taken over by italics, but there again ambiguity easily arises. We italicize for emphasis (of several kinds) as well as to show that we are talking about words themselves or about some special use made of them. In speech, of course, many of these subtleties can be handled by intonation and pauses, though not with high uniformity or equally well by all speakers.

At places in these essays, quotation marks will necessarily be

Meta-semantic Markers

given an inordinately heavy task to perfom. This there is no avoiding. In all interpretation work we have to be able to hold up words and phrases for separate and special attention, and we have to do our best to indicate our attitudes to them and to their meanings. It is somewhat absurd, indeed, that writers have not long ago developed a notation system for this purpose which would distinguish the various duties these little commas hanging about our words are charged with.

I have therefore experimented in my books since 1942 with a range of special symbols to take the place of the usual quotation marks. They are small letters placed, as quotation marks are, about the words, the phrases, and the sentences they single out. I continue this experiment here. A key to this notation follows. It will be found in practice, I believe, that two glances at the key are enough to prepare the reader to recognize, without consulting it anew, what I suppose myself to be doing when I use the notation. It gives us a compact means of commenting on the handling of language—more comprehensible, less ambiguous, and less distracting than the usual devices of parentheses qualification, and discussion. I believe it will abridge both the optical and the intellectual work of the reader.

KEY

ʷ____ʷ   indicates that the *word*—merely as that word in general—is being talked about. The marks are equivalent to "the word." For example, ʷtableʷ may mean an article of furniture or a list.

ʳ____ʳ   indicates that some special use of the word or phrase is being *referred* to. The marks are equivalent to, "Please refer to the place in the passage we should have in mind here." For example, ʳNatureʳ for Whitehead is not Wordsworth's ʳNatureʳ.

?____?   indicates that our problem is, What does this word say here? (Not whether anything it seems to say is

Meta-semantic Markers

acceptable or not.) The marks are equivalent to "Query: what meaning?" There is no derogatory implication. Most ?important? words are, or should be, in this situation.

!_____!   indicates surprise or derision, a "Good Heavens! What-a-way-to-talk!" attitude. It may be read !shriek! if we have occasion to read it aloud.

nb_____nb   indicates that how the word is understood is a turning point in the discussion, and usually that it may easily be read in more than one way or with an inadequate perception of its importance. The sign is short for *nota bene*.

sw_____sw   indicates that the reader is invited to consider Something that may be said With. The marks are short for "Something said With." It is useful when we need especially to remind ourselves of the very different things that may be meant by the words we are using.

i_____i   indicates that other senses the word may have in other occurrences may *intervene*. The marks are equivalent to "Intervention likely." By extension—

di_____di   would mean further "Danger! Watch out!" and

hi_____hi   would mean "helpful intervention." In contrast, a word or phrase to be read as having no relevant relation to any other senses in other places, actual or possible, could be written

t_____t   to mean "technical term" defined and fixed in this employment.

Lastly I will use the mark =, equivalent to, to indicate that the words or phrases it links are to be taken as having the same ?meaning? for the purposes in hand. This escapes the unfortunate suggestion that whatever the first is talking about !really is! the second. The usual device is to write (*i.e.*,＿＿＿), which too often carries the suggestion that somehow we have no need to ask ourselves what the second explanatory word or phrase is itself standing for here. An equally troublesome device is to add (or ＿＿＿), which commonly offers us a dangerous, if usually a crude, ambiguity. $^{sw}Or^{sw}$ then may be presenting an alternative thing or just another *name* for the same thing.

Extensions and refinements of this typographic device will be readily contrived by those who appreciate its economy and convenience. For example:

^{m}＿＿＿^{m} = metaphor whose transposition route invites exploration.

^{et}＿＿＿^{et} = etymon suggestive if not determinative.

^{D}＿＿＿^{D} = cited from a major Dictionary.

Contents

BEYOND

Prologue

The Dictionary (that inestimable successor to Holy Writ) tells us that a prologue is "especially a discourse or poem introducing a dramatic performance." I should perhaps admit that the differences between discourses and poems have not become as plain to me as I would wish. However, that the scenes which follow are essentially a dramatic performance seems right. Or, rather, a dramatic entertainment—an invitation offered to my readers to join me in entertaining certain notions, if only briefly. A number of works, from among the greatest, enter in various guises (whether *dis*guises or not is, partly, what the play is asking). They there confront one another. Being what they are— the spiritual ancestors: springs, headwaters, for the Helleno- centric and Judaic traditions, sources of our world and our very selves—what they do to one another, through the selected aspects I try to exhibit, provides the dramatic engagement. What the outcome may be is not to be presented here. If it could be set down (*down* is the word) the play would be needless. There will be more to these interactions and exchanges than any summary could report.

But a prologue can suitably alert the spectators, and list for them things to look out for. It can disown irrelevant aims and discourage inappropriate expectations. I would do these things here in a somewhat indirect, if not covert fashion. It is fitting

3

Beyond

for the chief relevances of a prologue to be recognized step by step as the play unfolds. These scenes are not a series of essays whose connections an introduction should expound. The scenes may look like essays, but only because the aspects of the *Iliad*, *Republic*, Job, other parts of the Bible, and *The Divine Comedy* that take part in this intellectual action can be most conveniently selected and presented so. Not my remarks on them but forces from the works themselves, I hope, will shape the plot. I am not primarily *discussing* these immeasurable beings. I am trying to invite them to speak and act for themselves.

A prologue, like a Spirit Calming Ceremony preceding a Noh play, may itself take a dramatic form. I offer this, then, as a sort of curtain-raiser, a short scene in which three of the most powerful intellectual forces of our tradition are brought face to face with one another. This short play tries to appraise both the situation from which they derive and what, severally and jointly, they can do about it. The title of this prelude might be "Sameness." Or "Recurrence"; or "Again" would do as well.

How can things be the same, or recur or come again? It looks a reasonable question. If we ask flatly: Can they? we get two vigorously opposed answers. One is brisk: "Why, yes of course!" The other is the sad "Never again!" It has sometimes seemed that Western philosophy originated in and has hardly been able to go beyond the contrast of these two answers and that Plato and Heraclitus must be refining them still—some would say in Elysium; others, in Limbo.

It will be noted that I have dressed these answers up with my "brisk" and "sad." I have made them much more emotional than they need be. In certain moods people will make them switch places: "yes" will voice resentment; "no," approval. It depends on the things and the answerers. But all these endless emotional and evaluative possibilities—likings and dislikings, hopes and fears, disappointments and deliveries—are, for this prologue, but incidentals: they supply background and off-stage music. Its action is between three strong and confident, and historically most contentious, rivals, offering each his own theory of sameness, each his account of how samenesses come about

4

Prologue

and of what saying that things are the same really means. These three bear old and familiar names honored by adherents, though sometimes somewhat abusively used by opponents. They are Realism, Nominalism, Conceptualism.

For Realists things are the same through participating in, sharing in, imitating, being occurrences of, manifestations of, instances of a Universal. Familiar but more ambiguous names that have been more used in place of *Universal* are *Idea* and *Form*. Often these are qualified by *Platonic*, since Plato, or the Socrates he presents to us, is supposed to have invented or discovered this account of sameness. It might be fairer to say that they found it in their language; that they developed into a philosophic instrument what had for ages been a handy device for asking questions about and exploring meanings. Commonly, the illustrations used are drawn from august or at least dignified topics. Socrates in the *Phaedo* takes the Beautiful, the Good, the Great, the Equal as his instances and holds that the safest answer to a question like What makes beautiful things be beautiful? is the occurrence in them of Beauty—in some high sense, the same in them all. As to other sorts of answers, his advice is that we should "distrust our experience and, as the saying is, 'be afraid of our shadow.'"

This was Socrates at seventy on the last afternoon of his life. But Plato is at great pains to show us also, in the *Parmenides*, a "very young" Socrates, seemingly fresh from happening on the Forms. He excites the admiration of Parmenides and Zeno by his eagerness. Parmenides sets out to demolish the doctrine and begins by asking Socrates whether "hair, mud, dirt or any other trivial and undignified objects" have Forms distinct from things we can handle. Socrates confesses that this thought has troubled him and, at times, forced him to retreat, for fear of falling into abysmal nonsense. That, says Parmenides, is because Socrates is still young. He will get over such fears when philosophy has taken firmer hold of him. What Parmenides does bring out are the difficulties, recognized ever since, in explaining the relation between an instance and that of which it is an instance: between

5

Beyond

the many *the*'s on this page and the one word THE.[1] Just *how* particular things partake of, or belong under, the Forms which make them what they are is not something explicable in terms of other relationships—relationships, that is, which are not themselves instances of it. The moral is that we have to accept this question as unanswerable. We have nothing deeper or clearer through which to answer it. All we can do is linger with it awhile until our feeling of the queerness of the situation we are in becomes familiar.

Dismayed at or repelled by this situation, Nominalists prefer to explain sameness through the names or labels that are applicable: all *the*'s may rightly be so called. It is the label which unites them and makes them *the*'s. Here, too, we may note as equally queer this dislike of the Unanswerable, this suspicion of it as "bordering unduly on the ineffable," this eagerness to rid the world of all but 'fully comprehensible' items, this supposal that it can be so rid. All this timorousness is hard to make out. What conception of 'fully comprehensible' and of 'fully comprehended', we should ask, do these thinkers enjoy?

What C. S. Peirce,[2] stepping aside from older philosophic language, called the "type-token ambiguity" is well exemplified by the printed page, the instance from which Peirce took his label. On this page you are now reading there occurs the letter *t*. There is only one letter *t*. And yet there are two of them in the word *letter*, three on the average in each line, and towards a hundred on the page. The one and only letter *t* is the *type*; the hundred or so occurrences are tokens of it. The same opposition

---

1. Typical problems for Realists to consider here are whether the many *the*'s on the page (configurations of ink) represent the printer's *the*, the linguistic *the* (which may appear in handwriting and in speech, actual and imagined), the mental *the*, which may be used in thinking though in no way uttered . . . in brief, all the troubles attending the word *word*. Happily, as we shall see, Nominalists and Conceptualists have equally all these troubles to attend to.

2. Charles Hartshorne and Paul Weiss, eds., *Collected Papers of Charles Sanders Peirce* (Cambridge, Mass.: Harvard Univ. Press, 1960), vol. 4, p. 423. Cf. C. K. Ogden and I. A. Richards, *The Meaning of Meaning* (New York: Harcourt, 1923), pp. 280–81.

Prologue

between what occurs and its occurrences can be noted, of course, wherever it is looked for. It is invaluable and indispensable. Language could not work without it. Nor could life go on. The human make-up is a type—actualized with differences in the writer and in whoever may read him. A cup of tea: that is one thing, the type; its tokens are drunk by the million. In most cases no inconvenience and no risk of confusion arise. Good, bad, indifferent: Lapsang Souchong at its most fragrant or stewed tannin, tea is tea; we can praise or condemn any token of it we taste. But in our praise or our condemnation itself the same opposition will be at work. We will be assigning tokens to types and recognizing types from tokens—just as in this paragraph we have been offering tokens of the type *type* and of the type *token*. In brief, meanings must be in some respect general if they are to be useful. Strict and utter uniqueness is merely a limiting notion: self-destroying, inapprehensible, and ineffable. An occurrence which was in no way *like* any other could not be an occurrence; nothing would be occurring. Uniqueness, in other words, is a matter of degrees of likeness in relevant respects. A unique occurrence is no more, we must conclude, than different in certain respects from any other.

By and large, few troubles develop from our use of the same word for the type and for the tokens. We see at once whether the letter *t* or an actual, individual *t* is being spoken of. Our concern is with what the tokens can convey, the meaning we take as type. I dealt further with this cardinal question in *Design for Escape* (New York: Harcourt, 1968, pp. 13, 100), especially with reference to semiotic translation between verbal, depictive, and enactive tokens. It is there suggested that the type-token relationship is of such consequence for theory of interpretation and theory of action that it might well be symbolized in printed discussion by the use of capitals for types and of lower case for tokens.

Among the topics for which confusion between token and type can readily arise and be, moreover, especially unfortunate, theory of meanings and its quasi translation or paraphrase, theory

7

of situations, endure a bad eminence. In both we have, as addressers and as addressees, to watch our steps as warily as we can. Thus a 'meaning' may be:

(1) An occurrence: a design, at one specific instant, in an addresser to communicate a specific message to an equally specific addressee. It is an event (dated and placed) hoping to induce, through a signal, the coming about of an exactly similar, reciprocal event in the addressee. (Such is often our presumption: we can probably agree that communicators would do well to replace the 'exactly' aim by something less demanding. Perhaps by "more or less" or by "very.") That is a token-use of "meaning"—a single specific occurrence.

(2) In the type use it should be recognized that thought about the type-token relationship remains mysterious to itself. Attempts to describe or to explain it, from Plato or Sankara on, are never satisfying—no doubt because we have, in these attempts themselves, to use this very distinction itself. We are concerned here with something so central to and so inseparable from thought that intelligence can hardly turn round in upon it, either to give some account of it or, more ambitiously, to account *for* it. "We cannot know the knower of knowledge" (*Brihadaranyaka Upanishad* [3]).

There has always been a suasive temptation to overlook or to refuse to accept the consequences of this continuing, indeed inalienable, control by types. The history of Nominalism is full of rich evidence. Most minds, perhaps all, however much or little they may be consciously aware of it, balance between the instance, *the labeled*, the easily identifiable *thing*, recordable, able to be attested in court at need, and the quite other sort of entity, the TYPE. Theory of semantics, with its "period-piece" predilections as to what the ways of science should, professedly,

3. In one translation, Max Muller's: "Thou couldst not see the (true) seer of sight, thou couldst not hear the (true) hearer of hearing, nor perceive the perceiver of perception, nor know the knower of knowledge. This is the Self, who is within all. Everything also is of evil." It is not surprising that "After that" the interlocutor "held his peace."

Prologue

be, has for more than a generation been heavily nominalistic. It has preferred (at any cost) to deal with easily identifiable items that could be entered in an inventory, presented in an account (bankruptcy proceedings, maybe, in the background?) rather than with unaccountable matters—to call them that—such as *invite* questioning and the kind of exploration which knows in advance that depth after depth will endlessly open to it. The virtue which Nominalism has really aspired to is tidyness, everything in its place. We can all respect this aspiration; it tries to defend us from our countless aberrations, and we can understand why, for innumerable Nominalists, this aim has been adventurous and challenging. But there are other intellectual invitations and some of them are (in the currencies here in question) more rewarding.

A fine recent prominent instance of nominalistic care and of concern for methodological decorum will be found in Nelson Goodman's bold and well-sustained *Languages of Art*. For him, talk about properties, characters, universals, classes, types is "informal parlance admissible only because it can readily be translated into more acceptable language." "I prefer," he says, "to dismiss the type altogether and treat the so-called tokens of a type as replicas of one another." [4] The continuing and indispensable help of the type in "readily be translated," and in "more acceptable language," and in any fuller account of "replicahood"—and, in fact and indeed, in any attempt to give some account of how every word and every letter (or every phoneme) in every utterance is *re*cognized is here typically overlooked. The necessities behind *sameness* are by no means so docile, so ready to vanish at the word "dismiss." (It is an unlucky word in such connections. See my *So Much Nearer*, pp. 13, 27.) As apology Goodman proffers:

In all this, the aptness of an emphasis upon labels, of a nominalistic but not necessarily verbalistic orientation, becomes acutely apparent once more. Whatever reverence may be felt for classes or attributes,

4. (London: Oxford, 1969), p. 131.

such classes are not moved from realm to realm, nor are attributes somehow extracted from some objects and injected into others. Rather a set of terms, of alternative labels, is transported; and the organization they effect in the alien realm is guided by their habitual use in the home realm.[5]

Such fancy metaphoric comment on metaphor tells its own story. Those labels are no more 'transported' (poor convicts) than classes are moved or attributes pumped out or in. All this is poetry bobbing up in the wrong place, in the midst, in fact, of an overly conscientious logic forgetful of what it serves. What we should not be forgetting, however, is that while such nominalistic scruples deter even the best-qualified inquirers, we are suffering heavy losses, on every cultural front, from our failure to look more deeply into what we are doing and into how we should be doing it.

As remedy we should start by recognizing that this mystery is at the heart of all comparings. We can and do use discernible samenesses and differences both in the token-fields and in the type domain. We perceive that a letter t is imperfect, and also we know—though in another way—that t is a different letter from i. These are all t's:

$$T \ T \ T \ t \ t \ t \ T \ T \ T \ t \ t \ t \ T \ T \ T \ t \ t \ t \ T \ T \ T \ t \ t \ t$$

and these all i's:

$$I \ I \ I \ i \ i \ i \ I \ I \ I \ i \ i \ i \ I \ I \ I \ i \ i \ i \ I \ I \ I \ i \ i \ i$$

With such things as letters, type-token ambiguities give us little trouble. We have in fact learned how to handle them in learning *how to read*. But there is another and a higher sense for *how to read*. We are concerned there, not with configurations of inkstains, but with meanings and situations. With these we are incessantly liable to mistake token-field matters for type-domain problems. As in trying to read some handwritings we keep taking defective instances for different letters, so in most of our communications our chief practical difficulties (as opposed to

5. Ibid., p. 74.

theoretical deficiencies: insufficiently refined concepts) come from confusions of these two orders. The miscreations thus induced cross with misapprehensions as to the jobs the sign elements in the sign complexes are undertaking. It is not surprising that misunderstandings play so large a part in our lives. The wonder is rather that they are not more frequent.

With this type-token opposition in mind it is tempting to speculate a little further. The printing illustration we have been using is one of the simplest, most easily analyzed cases that can be found. For convenience in computer use, less and less confusable code elements will no doubt be devised while, at the same time, briefings for computers are developed, enabling them to handle more and more complex code systems. Some sort of compromise between these two trends will be arrived at. This illustration can serve us here as a type specimen.

Every token, we can assume, will—given powerful enough microscopy—be found to be, in some respect and in some degree, different from any other. No two handwritings, no two voices, no two pairs of ears or eyes deal with words in quite the same way. Make the mesh fine enough and differences will appear. Nonetheless, each member of a token set, through differing from its fellow members, represents a type, and it is the type so represented which matters to meaning. Somehow we allow for these differences (within limits) and through the token apprehend the type. Thus, on the telephone, despite the noise in the channel and the peculiarities of the instruments through which the signal (the *token* stream) comes to us, we get the bonding *type*, and thence, maybe, the message. The message is what we are concerned about. In a similar way, when we rephrase ?what we have to say? we can regard the meanings of the rephrasings as tokens of that single coercive though questionable ?what we have to say?—and pass thence to a meaning as type. As we tolerate imperfections in a handwriting, in our interlocutor's pronunciation, in the telephone signal, in our hearing and vision, so, too, we tolerate obscurity, vacuity, and pleonasm—acceptable defects in ~redundancy~ what we receive as token phrasings. Our concern is with what

Beyond

the tokens can convey, the meaning we take as type. Going yet a step further, the situations dated and placed, within which and under the control of which communications are attempted, must equally be regarded as tokens. Every instance of a SITUATION that gives meaning to something that is said is—as an event, an occurrence, an occasion—a token. Here again we are only derivatively concerned with the actual and more or less unique complexes of dated and placed circumstances (the tokens). It is the SITUATION they exemplify and represent (their type) which is the guide we question as to what is being said and what it is we may have to do.

All this is true enough. Yet we ourselves, as tokens, have ever to deal, immediately, only with tokens, and be to others only tokens: tokens fearing or hoping as much even as Job, himself, that they are radically unable ever to be confronted with their type.

In between Realists and Nominalists stand Conceptualists. Sameness for them arises, they might say, not from the shared Universal or the appropriate replicahood of the label, but from correspondence with concepts, representational mediators, mental or neurological.

And yet, with every word through which they may say so, both the pervasion of the type and the replication of the token-label are equally inevitable. For indeed the central original question, What is sameness? remains unsolved in all three positions. Jointly, perhaps they illuminate it somewhat. Severally, each quite patently begs it. What is it to *share*, to be *appropriate*, to *correspond?* These are questions that have to be recognized as reappearances in various disguises of the old unanswerable sameness-with-difference problem.

With sameness, of course, as these hyphens indicate, belongs difference. Neither can work without the other. As we phrase our sentences, however, there are subtleties of appeal [6] to our

6. An interesting branch of syntactic semantics would concern itself with these subtleties—in emphasis, suasive effect, degree of confidence in utterance, et cetera—between, say, swbadsw and swnot goodsw, swpresentsw

audience (without and within) which often distinguish ^{sw}not different from^{sw} and ^{sw}the same as^{sw}, ^{sw}not the same^{sw} and ^{sw}different^{sw}. But strictly or $^{?}$logically$^{?}$, as we say, or for a simple computer, the two are a binary pair. They are, it seems likely, the most indispensable of all the tools of rational treatment, the tools without which none of our other tools can be contrived. Why, then, should it be so hard to say anything useful about them? Why does it seem maladroit, unmannerly, and even *presque cad*[7] to drag up any such question? There may be sound reasons—though not reasons which are easy to set forth and convey.

It will be noted that our play is beginning to take on a queer appearance: that of an attempt at the answering of an Unanswerable, the apprehension of an Inapprehensible, the explication of an Inexplicable. . . . Traditionally, of course, recognition that *X* is incomprehensible has not deterred people from attempting to comprehend it. Rather the contrary, indeed. Such recognitions serve as the stringing of the bow. In the outcome, what is shifted may well be what goes under the name of comprehension. So here. After formulations such as *That wherewith we inquire will not serve inquiry into inquiry* or *The work it can do is the explication of the hypothesis,* we take to looking for analogies, parallels, parables, metaphors, similes—to find, then, always sameness-difference back again in, and on, our hands. We have not overcome the problem, but we may have come to be on better terms with it.

---

and ^{sw}not absent^{sw}—*taken in concrete, sufficiently explanatory, actual discourse.* It would show that our linguistic resources for handling even such a fundamental matter as the contradiction-contrariety contrast have not yet been adequately studied. Among recent explorations may be mentioned C. K. Ogden's *Opposition.* In practice we manage these distinctions with great skill, but hardly anyone seems to have tried to analyze the *rationale.* The relatively simple logical problems were worked out and expounded long ago—largely by Aristotle—but the rhetorical and vehicular aspects still await sustained attention.

7. From a label on a *complet* in a tailor's window in the Rue de Rivoli, ca. 1938: *Très chic. Un peu snob. Presque cad.* What foresight of the shape of things to come!

Beyond

These similes, high (how encompass the All?) and low—indeed down to the ground, as with bootstrap lifting—recondite or familiar, farfetched or homely, all set us searching for the principle: the common source whereby they seem to help us to understand our situation. Their very diversity pushes the communality further up into the abstract in a way to make us revere the more than superb daring of Shelley's "Pinnacled dim in the intense inane." (To be trusted to understand *that* is truly restorative and Promethean.) Among these parables some look like etymonic puns—the endless paronomastic play of the Dictionary. For example, consider the word *term*. Any discourse is *limited* (given its bounds) by the terms (meanings, expressions) it employs. The units of which it is composed settle (determine) how much it can cover—as choice of center and radius fix circumference. What we begin with—our choices of samenesses and differences, our operative meanings—decides (cuts thoroughly, cuts down) where we will extend to, how far and in which directions. And it is from these limits that we may learn what those originative, creative choices were. In our beginnings will be found our end and from our end we may discover our beginnings—and in all the senses of *end* from terminus to purpose.

With this last word we step into theology. Realism, Conceptualism, Nominalism become no longer merely logical positions, claiming as such to be neutral as regards man's true being, the possibility of his immortality, and his relationships to other beings; they show themselves as, in fact, decidedly partisan. It is true that devices can be excogitated which disguise these trends. While discarding "the strange doctrine of abstract ideas"—whether as a Realist or as a Conceptualist might frame it—Bishop Berkeley, for example, can make his Nominalism seem pious doctrine by having ideas "imprinted on the Senses by the Author of nature." In general, special cases apart, Nominalists have been the "No Nonsense!" party, impatient of what they have deemed metaphysical lumber, Realists (better called, perhaps, Platonists) the party of those readiest to welcome strangeness, and Concep-

Prologue

tualists the middle-minded travelers unwilling to commit themselves to any extreme position.

To describe them so, in terms of their fears—Nominalists not wanting to be taken in, Realists not wanting to be left out, and Conceptualists hoping to avoid both dangers—is to make this great controversy largely an affair of diverse temperaments. That it has so often been marked by merciless intolerance fits with this. So does the inconclusiveness of the outcomes. Historically, the debate flares up and dies down rather as though the participants at first had high hopes and then came to despair of being persuasive. Such situations develop fierce repugnancies, strong enough to make the antagonists unable to conceive one another's positions. Socrates put this vividly. After warning Crito to be careful and not say anything he doesn't really believe, he goes on: "I know there are never many who think like this, and that those who do and those who don't can't help despising [feeling contempt for] one another." [8] Despise, feel contempt for—not too strong a description of how Realists and Nominalists have often regarded one another's views on universals. More than a mere wish to defend one's own position appears; an active need to disparage the opponent's motives and habits of mind takes part. Indications, these, of the moral-volitional components in these choices. It is interesting that such attitudes do not infect the earliest phases of thought about universals; they are absent in Plato's discussions—notably in the *Parmenides*—and in Aristotle. Later disputants have too often shown no such good manners.

Another characteristic of this oldest and most central of philosophic controversies is the queer remoteness from other issues in which it has been conducted. As Robert Hutchins [9] has well brought out, the problem of the universal, quite unlike most

8. *Crito* 49DE. The point concerned is what is perhaps the most original of all Socrates' moral inventions: the doctrine that it is never right to return a wrong, or to defend oneself against a wrong, by threat of retaliation. See my *Why So, Socrates?* (London: Cambridge, 1964).
9. Introduction to Chapter 96, "Universal and Particular," in *The Great Ideas: A Syntopicon of Great Books of the Western World*, vol. 2.

other philosophic inquiries, "seems to have the character of a professional secret." "The various solutions," he goes on to remark, ". . . are so many esoteric doctrines, each with its own sectarian name. The initiated can distinguish themselves from the novices by their proficiency . . . the outsider . . . may be completely left behind, wondering as much about how the question arose as about the meanings of the conflicting answers."

A partial explanation is that the Logicians who took over did not like to admit failure. This and the previous characteristics may be connected. Psychology has had something to say about the flight from actuality that may accompany defeat. And Logicians, it is observable, from Aristotle on, have been signally unable, for one another and for the laity, to say what Logic is. As Bertrand Russell delightedly pointed out—to Tarski, Carnap, Willard Van Quine, Gödel, and a few others who had met to decide just this—they deserve to be sacked for not knowing what they are doing.[10]

In more than one respect, Nominalism pairs off with Logic, Realism with Metaphysics, Conceptualism with Psychology. The Logician, preoccupied with technique of proof and more abstracted, professionally, than any others from the accidentals of actuality, can willingly labor at his own mystery within an extremely low cognitive vacuum, his being a ?formal? study. The Metaphysician, on the contrary, his polar opposite, ideally takes all knowledge as his concern. In the Western tradition, an insatiable thirst for every sort of instruction has, from Plato and Aristotle onwards, been traditionally a sign of the philosophic mind. Not the mere acquisition of the knowledge, but the finding of an intelligible order in or for it has been the Metaphysician's aim. Inevitably, this makes him early acquainted with, indeed overfamiliar with, unintelligibility. He learns to tolerate it more easily than others. He grows accustomed to high pressures from incomprehensibles. F. H. Bradley poignantly noted that "his pursuit condemns him, he may complain, himself to herd with

10. In 1940, in 9 Kirkland Place, Cambridge, Mass., at the end of a day spent in fruitlessly discussing that problem.

Prologue

unreal essences and to live an outcaste from life." [11] To such a one universals (which make the Logicians so "cough in ink and wear the carpet with their shoes") are his life breath. In between, the psychologist (of the William James variety) accepts his own mind, and by analogy the minds of others, as his more than sufficient field. Noting his own fluctuations, he can hope to understand both Nominalist and Realist better than they can one another. In a measure he has been both. In another sense than that of Aquinas, for him, knowing something is a way of becoming it; or, rather, to have been is a way of having known.

With such experience and the inclination to experimentation it gives him, he is ready to play imaginative games with possibilities. And he need have no more than temporary attachment to his conjectures. William James is our exemplar in that unwearying play. And it is he who will best remind us of what thinking, and the selection of likenesses with differences through which it proceeds, is for.

I confess that I do not see why the very existence of an invisible world may not in part depend on the personal response which any one of us may make to the religious appeal. God himself, in short, may draw vital strength and increase of very being from our fidelity. For my own part, I do not know what the sweat and blood and tragedy of this life mean, if they mean anything short of this. If this life be not a real fight, in which something is eternally gained for the universe by success, it is no better than a game of private theatricals from which one may withdraw at will. But it *feels* like a real fight,—as if there were something really wild in the universe which we, with all our idealities and faithfulnesses, are needed to redeem; and first of all to redeem our own hearts from atheisms and fears. For such a half-wild half-saved universe our nature is adapted. The

---

11. *Essays on Truth and Reality* (London: Oxford, 1914), pp. 13–14. I add his footnote: "I may perhaps illustrate this by transcribing one of those notes in which, some twenty years ago, I used to attempt to fix my passing moods. 'The shades nowhere speak without blood, and the ghosts of Metaphysic accept no substitute. They reveal themselves only to that victim whose life they have drained, and, to converse with shadows, he himself must become a shade.' "

Beyond

deepest thing in our nature is this dumb region of the heart in which we dwell alone with our willingnesses and our unwillingnesses, our faiths and our fears. As through the cracks and crannies of caverns those waters exude from the earth's bosom which then form the fountain-heads of springs, so in these crepuscular depths of personality the sources of all our outer deeds and decisions take their rise. Here is our deepest organ of communication with the nature of things; and compared with these concrete movements of our soul all abstract statements and scientific arguments—the veto, for example, which the strict positivist pronounces upon our faith—sound to us like mere chatterings of the teeth.[12]

Indeed, we may marvel at the confidence, as of folk terribly at ease in Zion, with which philosophers can in their argumentative preoccupations forget what they are about. Why should anyone be attempting rebuttals of others? What is their thinking in the end for?

The continuing theme, the labyrinth's clue, is this Why: this pursuit of the Unanswerable. What it would be if found may be intimated, hinted at, in countless ways. None of them do more than offer the mystery to us again. In them all, whether as discourse or as poem, with more or less self-recognition, Knowledge turns upon itself to admit itself to be ignorance. There clings to this confession of ignorance more or less acknowledgment of guilt. I once (in *Practical Criticism*), risked the phrase "the enormity of our ignorance." This won me a revealing gesture from the writer who, in *Ash-Wednesday,* for example, had seemed to me most likely to see what was implied. In quoting it, he appended *sc.*: "the enormity (*sc.*) of our ignorance" as though he might be encountering a solecism. Whether that suggestion was intended I did not find out.

However, two major, shaping positions, for me, interact here: the interdiction figured by the forbidden fruit and the Socratic tenet that Knowledge—could we attain it—would be Virtue. The

12. No. 425 in Robert Bridges' anthology *The Spirit of Man* (London: Longmans, Ltd., 1969). He notes: "This extract from 'The will to believe' was chosen for me by his brother, my friend the novelist."

18

Prologue

two, when truly coactive, are more capable of collaborating than either may seem apart. Contemplation of Eve's trespass, though in some it leads to "spitting from the mouth/The withered apple seed," can set its hand to the same task Socrates recommends to Phaedrus: "I am not yet able, as the Delphic inscription has it, to know myself; so it seems to be absurd, when I do not as yet know that, to inquire into extraneous matters." What he is setting aside here as postponable is rationalistic explanation of myths—such as that of the Tree. He is advising Phaedrus that to find out how not to be mistaken as to the kinds of knowledge most needful is the overruling task. And if the philosophy prayed for at the close of the dialogue is the offspring of wonder, and though, when young, it is cognitively omnivorous, its end is to learn how to choose.

Choice thus brings us back to the two principles, the two processes of putting together and setting apart, of which Socrates is a lover (*Phaedrus* 266B). To those skilled in such decisions about sameness and difference, he has hitherto given the name *dialecticians*. "Whether the name is right or wrong, God knows." But any so skilled he "follows after and will 'walk in his footsteps as if he were a god.'" And his aim is "to know whether I am a monster more complicated and furious than Typhon or a gentler and simpler creature to whom a divine and quiet lot is given by nature." [13]

What seems certain about this inquiry is that theories of sameness and difference can further it only by helping us to see more distinctly what we are doing. They are not candidates among which we have to choose; they are variously useful ways of approaching our choices as to how we combine and divide. Sameness-difference as an ultimate opposition must use more than one approach. To compare them is to examine, in a per-

13. *Phaedrus* 230A, H. N. Fowler's translation, Loeb Library. Paul Shorey's expansion may be compared: ". . . find out if I can whether my real self is the complex, passionate, smoke-blinded Typhon huge ending in snakey twine of appetites that I sometimes seem to be, or a simpler, gentler, humbler, clear-eyed creature by my true nature participant in the grace of God," *What Plato Said* (Chicago: Univ. of Chicago Press, 1933), p. 199.

Beyond

spicuous type specimen or exemplar, other sets of necessary oppositions: those between what we see and how we see it (the Homeric and the Platonic views of living), between what is said and how it is said (Book II of the *Republic* and the poem of Job), between any utterance and what it would utter.

As all know, ?the same thing? (so to call it) may be represented in different ways; and those ways themselves may mean different things as the fields, the settings, differ within which they are taken.

This situation, this necessary conjunction and opposition of an utterance and what it would utter, we cannot escape from; it is instanced again in every attempt we make to account for it. We deal with realities only through representations of them, and we need all the aids we can be given in remembering this.

Among such aids a pair of terms [14] introduced for the discussion of metaphor may be generalized (though with some change of sense) and be useful. Let ^{sw}what is to be said^{sw} be the Tenor, and ^{sw}the way of saying it^{sw} be the Vehicle; and their relation be represented as $\dfrac{\text{Tenor}}{\text{Vehicle}}$ $\left(\dfrac{T}{V}\right)$, as though the Tenor were a passenger riding in some sort of car. The image may usefully remind us that the events, the situations, we are dealing with have vector character: the utterance is trying to go somewhere. Setting it out so, we may the more conveniently bear in mind that we apprehend any V (and thereby, we would hope, *its* T) through comparing with other V's.

In my parenthesis I wrote "*its* T" to bring out a question. In practice we take for granted that one and the same T may have a variety of V's—indeed, a considerable number of them more or less fitting, appropriate, *serviceable* (our choice of words here is, of course, itself an instance of what it is discussing). Looking closer, thinking through a better lens, we will be likely to conclude that any change from V_1 to V_2 will in some respect and to

14. See I. A. Richards: *Interpretation in Teaching*, 2nd ed. (New York: Humanities, and London: Routledge, 1973), p. 121 and Chapter 8, and *Philosophy of Rhetoric* (London: Oxford, 1936), Lectures 5 and 6.

Prologue

some extent (important or not) result in, entail, *convey* a different
T. As he changes from one car to another, the passenger becomes
in some respect and degree different.

Nothing could possibly be more familiar to us all than all this.
It is instanced, illustrated, in all our perceptions or recognitions
of everything. What we do not sufficiently consider, however, are
(1) the degree to which any V takes its character from the
settings in which it occurs and (2) the degree to which it is
shaped by other V's which (in that setting) are or are not *sub-
stitutable* for it—able or not to replace it in this or that respect.
The process of prehending a V, of selecting, deciding between
ways to take it, is almost entirely (1) a noting of what comes
with it (before and after) in the unit to which it belongs and
(2) a recognizing of its compatibilities and *in*compatibilities with
other V's which might be offered. This noting and recognizing
may be explicit or tacit: supported by conscious examination and
experimental trial or merely assumed, with a latent readiness to
observe and to accept or reject if called upon. Change what
comes with it (1), and its relations to other possible and impossible V's (2) are changed.

I have put this as though with the hearer, the reader, in mind;
but it holds, too, of the speaker, the writer. He, too, is guided
(1) by what comes (and can and/or must come) with it in the
unit and (2) by the substitution field. In any more or less suc-
cessful instance of communication, addresser and addressee are
guided alike.

These cardinal truths, these hinges of all thought, haunt our
every reflective remark. We are prone to regard them as offering
chiefly threats to communication, and neglect to notice the immense services of the flexibilities they afford. Did these fundamental conditions of utterance not hold, how miserably limited
would be our powers; how little we could think of, and how little
would be what we can receive and somehow, with luck, convey.

So ends my curtain-raiser.

1

Some Vectors in the *Iliad*

Early in the *Iliad* (I, 188–222) Achilles is seen in two minds, "divided in counsel." Agamemnon has just threatened to come himself to Achilles' hut and take away fair-cheeked Briseis, Achilles' prize of honor. Should he now draw his sword and put an end to Agamemnon? As he is drawing it, down from Olympus comes Athene, unseen by any but him, and takes him by his golden hair. He turns about and knows her, and her eyes are terribly bright. He asks her what she has come for. She answers that Hera has sent her to tell him to hold down his anger. She adds that glorious gifts, three times as great as his present loss, will come to him through this affront. Achilles obeys.

This episode, if we should call it that, presents a most convenient and, I believe, both testing and testable example through which we may consider how we should read not only Homer but much else. It has the further advantage of bringing us into direct contact with recent Homeric studies in aspects which best illustrate some wide-spreading trends in contemporary scholarship.

The doubt as to whether it should be described as an *episode* or not concerns what I take to be a searching question, in whose

Some Vectors in the *Iliad*

light matters of perspective and connection often appear with increased clarity. It asks, What may be a minimal, irreducible *action*—in Aristotle's sense—for Achilles? Granting gladly that Athene's intervention here may offer tempting opportunities for expansion, elaboration, and dramatic enrichment, is it necessarily, essentially, and indispensibly a part of that action? Or is it, as the word *episode* would suggest, something which comes in besides? Which leads into an even deeper question: What can the intervention do *for* and *to* our view of Achilles' character?

We may be ready to regard such questionings and their discussion as displays only of whimsey. If not, several dramatic perceptions grow clearer and solider as we reflect.

(1) Athene, self-betrayingly, misconceives Achilles. She supposes that those gifts to come will weigh with him—in this matter of an outrage to his honor—as they certainly do not. In Book IX, when Odysseus details what Agamemnon will give as amends, Achilles rejects them utterly in one of the most revealing speeches ever conceived. And in Book XIX when Agamemnon offers his gifts again, Achilles' disdain for them is as palpable and downright. He is a greater and deeper being than Athene can take in. However much of a goddess of victory and the arts she may be, she is but a child compared with him. She can thus serve him excellently *as a foil*.

(2) His seeing her when no others can (she arranges that) singles out his semidivine status enhancingly. It is worth noting that Thetis is the only one of the goddesses worthy of being Achilles' mother.

(3) Her taking him by the hair and the terrible flash of her eyes give added force to the calm with which he addresses her.

(4) In letting his sword be and in only reviling Agamemnon and warning him of what is to come, he accords with her directions. But by that he loses nothing of his superiority. She has intervened for her own and Hera's purposes—which do neither of them any credit. That he lets her have her way, knowing of her vindictiveness and her claims to foreknowledge (that paralyzing fiction), does not diminish him. It is only the most respectable

sort of prudence. It may be noted that in her last intervention—when she pushes in disguised as Deïphobus to help Achilles by her treacheries (XXII, 226)—she does come near to lessening Achilles' honor. But by then he has become too invincible for her trickeries to matter.

These are a sample of the perceptions which, I think, reflection on this incident of Athene's first intervention will continually develop and confirm. In considering their justice, the old formulary of scholarship still holds and applies. What is needed to validate any judgments on such matters is an equal balance of outer and inner testimony. We must be as aware as we can be of the text and of how it has been taken. Without that, any inner appraisal has too little to rely on and to check itself against. On the other hand, inner appraisals (of all sorts and often of undeterminable source) enter into our awareness of the text and of its interpretations from the first, and, in more than a few ways, some of them are selectively decisive. One of the advantages of returning, more than once and after considerable intervals, to a great work is that we may be helped so to realize how we ourselves have been changing in the intervals and how inevitably the work, too, then changes for us. We may catch sight of some of our initial misappraisals. They readily mislead; can, indeed, quite prevent our receiving the outer testimony—the text and how it has been taken—with sufficient faithfulness. And yet that outer testimony, *by itself* (could such an impossibility be conceivable), would be powerless. The outer component comes before our judgment (qualified or not) as before a Court of Appeal. Radically, our inner testimony is what it seeks.

Such a view, in today's terms, may seem absurdly obvious. We are perhaps so familiar with and convinced of the merits of "the exploratory position" that it may seem silly to stress it. But, traditionally, very different stances have, more often than not, been expected—of the scholar and of his audiences. His prime business, it has been conceived, was to find and declare the Truth, which his audiences had to take in, preserve and treasure. Neither master nor pupil has usually been at all invited to see himself as

venturing new, much less original, interpretations. And for under-
standable reasons. In ages when a Creation (with a fairly recent
date) and an appointed End of the World could frame man's
thinking, a 'finality' as regards bits and pieces of the Whole
seemed easily attainable. But any speculations we can today
entertain as to 'finalities' (in this as well as in other and very
different senses) live only in a developing universe whose history,
striking characteristics, and present trends seem a tissue of unimaginably strange and reckless experimentations, many of them
—perhaps most, we may suspect—blind, dead-ended, noncontribu-
tory. (This may, of course, be a biased, contemporary biologic
guess, a freak of current fashion.) However, innovation—and not
only because human inventiveness has been snowballing of late
and without much direction—comes to look very like a biologic
principle: innovation under the control of outer and inner testimony. From the cell up, the living being has to do more than get
its informative directives right and obey them; it has its selective
duties, too. It has to choose ways of adjusting itself and serving
its collaborators which will best suit with its place in the relevant
order as that is reflected in its own being. In such ways the
favored procedures even of minute textual interpretation are influenced by the current world picture—whether or not the practi-
tioners can be fully conscious of what is shaping their thought.

Such an over-all picture now serves as the frame (contrasting
vigorously with earlier frames) within which we have to form our
critical estimates of men's conceptions and depictions (through
the millennia) of the superhuman forces (outside *and* within
them, before them *and* behind them) with and against which
they have somehow to pursue their ways. Among these conceptions and depictions, the Olympian divinities have a role and
character which has been recognized from relatively early times
as by no means simple or obvious. Both in their extraordinary
individualities and in the strange contrasts they point to the human figures subject to their highly arbitrary whims, they are
among the most challenging or even baffling of poetic creations.
How they came into being has commonly remained a mystery

to any who cared to raise that daunting question. Those who have ventured answers have usually constructed them not so much from the *Iliad* as from current speculations on the creative process combined with hypotheses about the origins and early histories of religions.

Among these products in recent times may be mentioned the view that more than we suppose of what may be labeled source literature of religion derives from the critical-satirical utterances of poets revolted by devotional acquiescences. More often than not, so we may indulge our fancy, poets who were original, protesting, outraged might have been (on their leave-visits from Elysium) aghast to find their destructive caricatures being worshiped as icons. In most ages, it has been assumed, gaps between self-critical, self-judging originators and the many-leveled masses of conformers will have been big enough for the wildest aberrations to have occurred.

Such extravagances invite a return to our distinction between outer and inner testimony. Here is a partially coincident, partially divergent account of it (from a slightly shifted viewpoint). It may help to give a more stereoscopic view of this problem of the interaction of components in interpretations. We have two beyond-reckoningly complex systems of recognitions to try to conduct

(1) the textual and circumstantial (outer) data mentioned above and especially as to how good readers have hitherto connected items one with another;

(2) our own (inner) uncertainties of experience—to which, after all, how we should take (1) cannot but be subject, since what meanings we find for it necessarily arise from, or through, (2).

In trying to order as best we can these two fields of forces (that is, to respond most entirely and least confusedly to them) we have two loyalties to reconcile: (A) the position we imagine our poet, 'Homer, or some substitute for him', to be devising and managing; (B) the position we would acknowledge to be *ours*. The probability that our view of (A) will be unduly, maybe distortingly, shaped by (B) should be a major restraint. In matters so fundamental as these the two loyalties are hardly separable. We only come by our own view of our position through our attempts to imagine the positions of others.

Back now to our type-specimen, Athene's intervention. No doubt our views of the Olympians—any human views of them except those that unifying Homerists of the last decade or so have been proposing—are likely to be tainted by one of the lowest of the vices: Envy, as Dante and his sources saw it. So much about the gods' activities resembles what unheroic, underexperienced, unreflective humans have habitually imagined and pursued as covetable: an unending, conscience-free, sportswomanlike billionaire existence. We do well, therefore, to be somewhat on our guard, in appraising them, against our counterreactions. Perhaps a recognized (and, if necessary, cultivated) ambivalence in our own attitudes and feelings towards their doings may be useful in approaching the questions that any close study of the roles of the Olympians in the *Iliad* should raise. On the other hand, their activities undoubtedly represent what the Good Life has seemed like to countless among the audiences and readers of the *Iliad*. Equally undoubtedly they have also conveyed, lent themselves as a vehicle for, a lively satirical-ironical criticism and repudiation of any such goings on as an end for man.

There is no doubt about this duality in the *receptions* the poem has been accorded. Such picturings of the desirable can make some mouths water as much as they can make other mouths purse themselves or grin. What vanities these Olympians have to indulge, what games they have to play to divert themselves and make their burdenless existence tolerable: snuffing up savors from burning thighs of oxen; watching cities being sacked (see Gilbert Murray's description of that ultimate horror in *The Rise of the Greek Epic*); waiting through endless battlings for that to happen they know beforehand must occur; pretending that by taking part they are preventing Fate from being flouted. As Cedric Whitman strikingly remarks, "Fate amounts to what the poet knows is in the scenario." To the poet his knowledge of that future gives *him* peculiar power; in that respect he is in charge of events. But to the gods what a dreadful handicap their fluctuating foreknowledge is; how nugatory it makes their pseudo action. It is a disqualification as trivializing as even their immunity from death. Their foreknowings and their immortality alike degrade the Olympians, as much as his mortality and his knowledge of it exalt the hero. For a modern reader the contrast can go some way towards offering a theodicy, towards reconciling us to our ignorance and to the inevitability of death. But it would be folly to attribute any such aim to the *Iliad*. That would be shutting our eyes to too much in it that we can plainly observe and know. It is in these connections that it is probably most necessary to distinguish between how the poem has been taken and what is involved in its design.

And yet the temptation to identify an impression the poem makes with what may have been active in its composition is terribly strong. I may illustrate it, I hope, from what I wrote in the introduction to my simplified version:

> In spite of the handicap of immortality and the ironic obliquities, the immortals are still personalities, true to themselves if to nothing else, and fully rounded. A remarkably definite family group is thus projected into heaven. That is a suggestive place for the first appearance of the parental "scene" and interesting evidence for the influence of the family constellation. It is as though the poet, or the poetic tradition, could find no better image for the governance of events than in memories of household dissensions a detached and highly observant child has witnessed.[1]

That registers, I still think, a faithful impression. I do not take it as having any bearing on how the *Iliad* came to be.

We may well—throwing ourselves for a while into a somewhat Olympian posture—enjoy much in the Olympian scene: its bickerings, triviality, frivolity, malice, selfishness, vanity, deceit, and heartless cruelty, concerned for their offspring though some of them are, taking it as a depiction on a glorifying screen of

---

1. *The Wrath of Achilles* (New York: Norton, 1950), p. 10.

much human behavior. That is its richly comic aspect. At the opening of Book IV, Zeus, expressly to mock and provoke Hera, says, with malice:

Menelaus has two of the goddesses for helpers, Hera and Athene, but they only sit still and look on while laughter-loving Aphrodite is always at Paris' side, keeping off fate; and now she has saved him when he thought he would be killed.

Twice, after similarly enraging Athene, Zeus suddenly smiles and remarks: "Take heart, my child, I am not as serious as I seem." The second time he says this is when he is sending her down from Olympus to lend a hand in the killing of Hector.

All this, headwaters, earliest known source for what we know as comedy, can be delicious. Need it prevent us from noting and responding to other aspects? The action of the *Iliad* begins with Apollo loosing shaft after shaft, first on the mules and swift dogs, then on the men, till day and night the pyres of the dead burned thick. Why? Because Agamemnon—against the will of the Greeks— has dishonored Chryses, Apollo's priest. (Agamemnon wants to keep Chryses' daughter as his prize of honor. Indeed, as he tells the whole gathering of the Greeks, he prefers her before Clytemnestra, his wedded wife, for she is as beautiful, as tall, as skillful in handiwork and as wise. Modern readers may perhaps think that this should be enough to earn him what he gets from Clytemnestra when he returns home.) It is with this slaughter of blameless Greeks, then, that the action opens. It ends with the story of another act of justice performed by Apollo, who is singled out as "best of the gods" and throughout the *Iliad* is accorded especially honorable treatment. Achilles, near the end of Book XXIV, persuades old Priam to take food after long fasting by telling him the story of Niobe: even she at last took food nine days after Apollo had shot down her six lusty sons and his sister, Artemis, their six sisters—all because Niobe had said that Leto had but two children and she herself twelve. Somewhere now, Achilles says, amid the rocks on the lonely mountains, Niobe, though turned to a stone, still thinks of what the gods did to her. But Achilles by then is no friend to Apollo, who killed Patroclus and tricked Achilles himself in his advance on Troy. And it is Apollo who, after the close of the *Iliad*, guides the arrow loosed by Paris that is to kill Achilles.

It would be easy to fill a long chapter with incidents that do little credit to gods and less still to the goddesses. Hera's seduction of Zeus, most diverting though it is, we may think deserves the thrashing he threatens her with. And Athene's cunning in tempting Pandarus to break the solemnly sworn truce—sworn, incidentally, before her among the other immortal gods—matches well with her meddling in Hector's last duel. It illustrates further the queer limitations set upon what even she can do. Looking like one of the Trojan spearmen, she goes up to Pandarus and says, "Wise-hearted Pandarus, why not let fly a swift arrow now at Menelaus and win great glory in the eyes of all the Trojans and King Paris most of all? What will he not give you to see Menelaus killed by your arrow?" She has, we note, rather material views on men's motives. As his arrow flies over men's heads, "the gods kept you in mind, Menelaus, then. Athene turned away the arrow as a mother will drive a fly away from her sleeping child. She guided it to where his armor was thickest, but right through it all the arrow went. It cut his outer skin only." Only a light though alarming wound, not Menelaus' death, was in the scenario. That the images of the swept-aside fly and the guiding of the arrow do not entirely articulate is characteristic. In Book V Athene does some more guiding. Pandarus, whom she beguiled, comes up against Diomed, who hurls his spear; "and Athene guided the spear upon his nose beside the eye and it pierced through his white teeth. So the stubborn bronze shore off his tongue at its root, and the spear point came out by the base of the chin." It is noteworthy in a poem so based on the use of formulas that there are hardly two woundings in it alike. The fanciful might conjecture that its hidden author was the great surgeon Machaon. "A surgeon is of more value than many fighting men" (XI, 515). But to return to the comedy aspect. When Diomed by Athene's instructions

(V, 133) has wounded Aphrodite in the wrist and her mother, Dione, has healed it, Athene and Hera, looking on, seek to anger Zeus with mocking words. "Aphrodite," says Athene, "has been after some Greek woman to get her to go with one of the Trojans she loves so much and while stroking her she has scratched her hand on the woman's broach." But at this Zeus merely smiles.

I have strung together these samples of the comic and the dismaying, the diverting and the horrific in the conduct of the gods with several aims in view: (1) To help in realizing how truly tremendous the task of unifying the *Iliad* would be. There can, of course, be many kinds as well as degrees of unity. The extremer modern unifying Homerist conceives the task very strictly. His design could not be more ambitious. It is to show how "the intuitive levels of imagery and divine machinery in the *Iliad* . . . reveal its soundness as the work of a single mind." [2] (2) To help in thinking about how the vastly diverse elements and structures in the poem can be combined to give—some of them—consentaneously consistent outcomes. (3) To help in asking whether certain modes of interpretation employed in endeavors to unify do not actually result in a less, rather than in a more, consistent poem. (4) To help in calling attention to some highly general considerations about, for example, what sorts of instruments used in such discussions can yield reliable or even examinable results. (5) To help in clarifying further, if possible, what has been sketched above as the collaborations (and oppositions) of outer and inner testimony.

(1) I have touched already above on the key problem: the nature of the inference from features observable in the poem to suppositions as to its mode of composition. I suggest here that almost all that we may say about how a poem was composed (above all, such a poem as the *Iliad*) is but a device (our traditional device) for describing what we find in it. Unifiers, of course, can agree to this, momentarily, without realizing that it should prevent their using their own hypotheses about how a

2. Cedric Whitman, *Homer and the Heroic Tradition* (Cambridge, Mass.: Harvard Univ. Press, 1958), p. 238.

mind works as arguments for ascribing features to the poem. The self-denying ordinances of the behaviorists and linguists have at least brought this out clearly. If we suppose we know how poets work, we introduce factors into our reading of a poem which can (and often do) distort our reading illimitably. Our remedy is to take ˢʷthe poet's mind in the act of creationˢʷ as a screen on which we can display what we observe of the behavior of the words before us, how they make sense or don't together. It is this which supplies our evidence. To reverse the inference, to argue from what we think we know about poets to what we will make poems mean and be, is, in fact, highly fallacious. Of course we will use our knowledge of other poems from other cultures in our reading of it. Not to do so would be stupid. But to do so is not the same thing as transferring our hypotheses as to how they have come to be and applying them to the highly different and peculiar problem of the coming into being of the *Iliad*.

The little that is known (as opposed to the vast amount of conjecture ventured) about the diversities of conditions under which works of art and cultural products in general are formed supports this recommendation. We have no experience (unless it is in what we find in the *Iliad*) of what a school of poetic composition (not a course in creative writing) through which rhapsodes were in long, continuous training, endlessly listening to one another's performances and seething with emulation, could do to their poetic output. Is it really hard to imagine institutions which in a few lifetimes could give any mode, extent, and degree of unity (internal connexities) that can be validly discerned in Homer. To say so is to forget what styles in many arts (notably including pottery) have produced; it is to forget how what we nowadays call a forger can, even in the most ʔindividualʔ traits, improve on a master.

(2) My string of samples of divine behavior raises, I hope, questions of validities of connection. These instances of ruthlessness, lack of scruple, pettiness, cattery, malice, et cetera can (with some strain) be combined in the comedy aspect to yield

exceedingly bitter contrasts to the relatively pure and exalted conduct of some of the mortals. They may be compounded with human heroism into savagely melancholy perception of the incomprehensible outcomes of endeavor. There are moments when to watch the President of the Immortals smiling in self-congratulation at his little joke is salutary and restorative. It can be a way of, as William James put it, "expanding the ventral and contracting the dorsal aspect of the frame." Or, while other imports are being considered, all this queer divine behavior can just be ignored. Anything can be temporarily ignored for the sake of something else—but not in the promotion of a treatment which aims at being more unifying than others.

It is not so easy and allowable to practice such selective neglect with some other styles of interpretation—those, for example, which find for these same gods' dealings with humans all sorts of profound metaphysical and metapsychological significances. For instance, when it is said that Achilles is present through "the whole middle part of the poem . . . there in the form of a translated Zeus, governing the phases of the long battle with his lightning; his whole character, state of mind, and relation to circumstances is enormously projected into the concrete image of the god." [3] Or, again, when it is said of the type-specimen episode with which I began: "When she [Athene] restrains him by the hair from killing Agamemnon, self-awareness, of a kind appropriate to the deity of the arts and intellect, is clearly implied. . . . The goddess is not an act of conscience, or a symbol of divine law, reproving violence or murder; she is the sudden self-realization of Achilles in the moment of stress, the visible symbol of the way he must, of his nature, conduct himself." [4] As to the things she is *not*, we should, of course, heartily agree. But as to what she *is* (this treacherous word almost cries out here for italics), we must, I think, as firmly dissent. So, too, when it is

3. Ibid., p. 230. On the same page the doings of these divinities are referred to as "facets of the divine nature" that "light up in response to the phenomena of the world." Surely we are here a long way from the actual *Iliad*.   4. Ibid., p. 231.

maintained that "the god in such scenes is the clear moment of insight and decision"[5] and that "As Homer has drawn her, Aphrodite is the predicative image of all Helen's deeds, attitudes and circumstances."[6] So, too, when it is said that "none of the others saw her" (Athene), it is "a plain hint that she is the projection, the pictorial expression, of an inward monitor."[7] The divine intervention may prompt a moment of insight and arouse Achilles' or Helen's fuller realization of their situations, but that is another matter. No one, I suppose, would doubt that Athene and Aphrodite may in these scenes be used to reflect or bring out the hero's or heroine's situation, or that this can be marvelously skilled and effective. Enthusiasm about their effectiveness is probably the source of these meta-methodological extravagations. They are misleading, however, if they make anyone forget that it is the Athene of the *Iliad*—not the "deity of the arts and intellect," but the goddess Zeus sends to make the Trojans break their oaths *first*[8]—who takes Achilles by the hair and that it is the Aphrodite who has just baffled Menelaus, and not some projection of Helen's nature and condition, who "brought a seat and put it for her facing Paris."

(3) I have hinted at the main source of my doubts under (2): the divinities are individuals, personalities as distinct—the chief of them—as the most fully developed of the heroes. As they are made over into objectifications[9] of states of mind, the losses seem to me to outweigh any gains. Their motivations, their

5. Ibid., p. 217.   6. Ibid., p. 225.
7. E. R. Dodds, *The · Greeks and the Irrational* (Berkeley: Univ. of California Press, 1951), p. 14.
8. It is worth noting that she is sent "to go her way into the dread din of battle," though the two hosts are sitting down peaceably together, except Menelaus, who is ranging about like a wild beast looking for Paris.
9. "Homer certainly did not invent this method of objectifying states into divinities; such a process must be one of the formative elements in the growth of any polytheistic religion" (Dodds, *The Greeks*, p. 222). It may be felt that a very wide gap between the largely unconscious processes through which divinities may be supposed by the anthropologist to grow into being and the conscious sophisticated use of adaptations from them in poetic invention is here being very lightly leaped over.

Some Vectors in the *Iliad*

tensions, their absurdities, which make them in some ways so beguiling, grow blurred along with the grimmer aspects which make them, in view of the responsibilities they claim and the privileges they enjoy, so detestable. No doubt the treatment the unifying Homerist employs does enable him to point out much that has not, to my knowledge, been remarked before. Few of his readers will have failed to recognize how much they have learned from him—not on this objectification front, but on many others—and be correspondingly grateful. Perhaps his theoretic machinery helped him in his perceptions. That will be its sufficient justification; but if, as I believe, it can hinder others, it can and should be dispensed with. What it has enabled can be secured otherwise.

(4) No one who has been engaged in such interpretive endeavors will be unfamiliar with the embarrassing thought that the explicative terms he finds himself using need at least as much elucidation as the matter he is employing them on. This can be a fruitful thought. Frequently such gain as may be made in the general tasks springs directly from some further questioning of such terms. These remarks are, of course, no more than a borrowing from the punning possibilities of ᵂtermᵂ. It is evident, I trust, that analysis and synthesis are limited by the capacities of the instruments through which they are attempted. H. G. Wells's remark about trying to cut an atom in two with a penknife comes to mind. If concepts such as are represented by symbols (unless finely qualified in some fashion) like "intuitive levels," "imagery," "divine machinery," "single mind," "unity," and "consistence" are used, the outcomes cannot (except episodically) be finer and more discriminating than the agents that produce them. To take these symbols up seriatim:

intuitive (mainly a negative): looking in on something *without* intermediaries, hence a claim for spontaneity and independence; thus evading, so far as feasible, the prime conditions of apprehension: the bonds of meaning;

levels: an exceedingly dubious and strangely unexamined

metaphor, used as stopgap in cases where critical analysis is not expected or invited;

imagery: very fertile source of confusions, being the most flexible and least controllable loose equivalent of ˢʷrepresentationˢʷ;

divine machinery: in this connection implying a subordination of the gods to the depiction of the humans. But that is not what most good readers have found in the *Iliad;*

single mind: none of us, looking into ourselves, can be at all safely sure of where our thinking, et cetera, ends. Those from whom we have learned seem to interpenetrate it throughout. We can even reasonably doubt whether a ˀsingleˀ (independent, self-sufficient, et cetera) mind is not an abstractive limitary fiction. It may be added that the highest instances of unity we know—for example, mathematics and the Dictionary—are the creations of unnumbered sequences of co-operative and respectful pupils. Possibly we would all be happier if more people became more aware of their dependencies as ˀselvesˀ on other ˀselvesˀ;

unity: philosophically the most central question, having its ramifications throughout all thinking. It divides into all sorts of connections which have to be discriminated and ordered so as to be as serviceable as possible to the problems in hand;

consistence: agreement with itself and with others relevant. The great question, of course, is how the agreement is obtained: by force (or threat of force) from *without* or by common *consent from within*—mutual understanding among the parties concerned. In poetic matters *consentaneity* would be a better word. Over this topic Plato's virtue, sophrosyne, rules.

(5) We come back so to the outer and inner testimonies. And we have, unless I am grievously mistaken, an interesting illustration in the work of the unifying Homerist, who has provided me with . . . I certainly can never say how much. In *Homer and the Heroic Tradition,* to my relatively uninformed eyes, there appears a magnificent example of command over outer testimony— over the text and relevant commentary, background data of every description and especially as to the history of how the *Iliad*

has been taken. One would expect that with the increase in the last hundred years or two in resources allocated to scholarship, with the mounting competition, with the increase in the numbers of talented researchers and in the means of making their reports mutually available,[10] the standards of performance in these old traditional fields would go up. But I did not foresee that I would read any book showing such impeccable command of the text, and of all other *outer* testimony relevant to it, before I could slip away to talk the thing over with Homer. Having said that and added my thanks, I have to turn to the question of our inner testimony.

As I have perhaps overstressed above, we are none of us sure where the most active presuppositions and presettings of our prehensions come to us from. They are not infrequently—as generation against generation can demonstrate—reactions from the conclusions of predecessors. Conceivably, Gilbert Murray (whom I mention *honoris causa*) and what he represents may have had not a little to do with the shaping of unifying Homerists. My point here is that sometimes extremely oversimplified oppositions—the *Iliad* as against an Old Testament or a *Divine Comedy*, for example—can take over and direct even a lifetime of argument. A truth in this matter is that, as yet, such comparisons call for the wariest walking. Each important product of any culture, every great work—most of them alertingly *singular* in power and far above all their derivatives—is probably as unique as anything can be, in its character and as to the conditions through which it came about. In many instances these originating conditions can only be guessed about from the evidence to be found in the work itself—an inevitably risky sort of guesswork, however much it may be supported and controlled by the converging evidence from archaeological, linguistic, and anthropological sources.

I preluded my suggestions about Athene's first intervention

10. We do well to reflect carefully upon what the services the computer is likely soon to be offering to scholarship may do for interpretation. That there may be dangers to watch out for may be hinted in the Jovial or Zeus-like suggestions of the little phrase, *do for.*

with a recognition that such discussions may be regarded as no more than displays of whimsey. The more what may be described as the relatively mechanical techniques of scholarship develop— the indices, the digests, the reference systems; all that computer handling both typifies and requires; all that makes scholars so often sigh for the leisures and simplicities of the horse-and-buggy epoch of their calling—the more all this advances, the more the distractive capacities of outer testimony mount. As the instrument panels, with their signals that just *cannot* be ignored, grow ever more complex and exacting, the threat offered to what I have called the inner testimony seems much more likely to increase than to diminish. I stressed above how subject to inner pre-hensions the selection and ordering of outer evidence must be; as we well know, this can much mislead. I should add here the sad note that patternings in the outer testimony, opportunities it can hold out for novel and striking notions, are among the most suborning of all the influences which can infect the contribution of inner testimony. Who with any wide experience in these fields does not know how easily symmetry, the invitations of elegance, of completion, of closure, of contrast, and the countless temptations of theory can silence the inner voice—which otherwise would be saying: "This will not do at all. Marshal your facts and their reinforcements as impressively as you may; another and more integrative perception negates them." What we have to fear, as theory follows theory and interpretations expandingly outdo one another and popularizers relay them as fast as they can, is that the whole enterprise of trying to understand great works will suffer disparagement, that the senatorial mind confronting the research councils as the need for cuts increases will conclude that it *is* all whimsey . . . and where will the libraries or their deputies of the future be then?

Yet, squarely face the question: What are we doing in trying to understand any great work?—and we must, I think, agree that it is from just such invitations to integrative perceptions that all the finer moral texture of living derives. Imaginative play? If that label for these deliberations should seem slighting, we must find a better. How do we weigh what, somehow, we can conceive of our nature against what of it is presented to us by those who have somehow, through an explorable process, been acknowledged to be the best judges? That is, I take it, our fundamental problem. As such it is perennial and recurrent. With its ramifications and banyanlike supports and new root searchings, it becomes any alerted mind's prime business. It can be described simply as the quest of what to be—again a matter of collaboration between outer testimony from the masters and our own developing inner witness.

As to who the masters are, the explorable process that has provided the list in our own culture—and probably in many others, in the Chinese certainly—is itself perennially before us for judgment. Reading any master is, of course, a process of being judged as well as of judging. It is surprising, and should maybe be comforting, that the ransacking of the past that has been accelerating through recent centuries has not as yet brought to light forgotten or buried masters who rank with the greatest. In some cases, as modern scholarship accumulates more evidence, it becomes harder to imagine how a great work came to survive. With the Book of Job, for example—to which the next chapter proceeds—that it became canonized is a puzzling problem, in view of what is becoming clearer about it and about the predilections of any probable canonizers. Possibly we should conclude that it was canonized through misapprehension. But this is only one of the many puzzles it presents.

The history of most great books shows them as having very often been praised for what may seem almost unimaginably wrong reasons. Mistakings, wrenchings, and distortions to an extraordinary degree seem to have been strangely frequent. How far this is a true picture, or how far it is an appearance produced through conditions in our contemporary scholarship, deserves to be pondered. Despite all this, the masters, on the whole, seem to have remained with a remarkable constancy in high favor. Cynical explanations have been offered. More to the point is that these great originators (on whom we should so gratefully admit our dependence) had, in addition to—or, rather, inextricably combined with—what they had to present, ways of presenting things (important or not) beyond the power of others. It is an interesting reflection that the most momentous perceptions have been perpetuated—and the survival of their vehicles secured—not because the perceptions themselves were readily communicable, or even acceptable or welcome to many, but because of the accompanying seductiveness, the inviting appeal of the vehicles. So, what Homer was to become to men—despite Plato's blind misapprehensions, as they may seem to us—hung less upon what he would say with the spear tip than upon the unmatched felicities of his ways of saying so much else: as though it were the carving on the chariot's rails rather than the hero who rode in it that won the battle; or the ornament on the pelean spear that counted rather than its weight or length or balance.

So too, maybe, with Job. It will be timely much later to try provisionally to consider what the vision of the heroic the *Iliad* created has done and may still do to man. We turn first to study the transcendently different versions of the heroic that the Book of Job has given us.

2

The Book of Job

My first close encounter with the Book of Job was also my first experience of the excitements and hazards of teaching. It was in a study group that met weekly to prepare its members to become leaders of discussion in other study groups within the Adult School Movement active under the influence of the Society of Friends. That dates back to 1908–10, when I was still a boy at school. As I was highly charged with revolutionary-atheistical sentiments by induction from Shelley and Swinburne, Jahveh (as the poet of Job notably refrains from calling him) was just what I wanted. I cannot conceive how those I harangued—with the indignation of an Elihu, though from an inverse of his position—took what I had to say. I remember only kindness and the finest spirit of tolerance. I had to conclude that I was not probably teaching much. I am not sure that I learned much, either—except perhaps about the power of preconceptions.

Swinburne had taken me to Shelley, who took me to Byron. *Cain* fitted in finely. I suspect that even then I was fond of quoting *Don Juan:*

Beyond

No more—no more—Oh! never more on me
    The freshness of the heart can fall like dew,
Which out of all the lovely things we see
    Extracts emotions beautiful and new;
Hived in our bosoms like the bag o' the bee.
    Think'st thou the honey with those objects grew?
Alas! 'twas not in them, but in thy power
To double even the sweetness of a flower.

No more—no more—Oh! never more, my heart,
    Canst thou be my sole world, my universe!
Once all in all, but now a thing apart,
    Thou canst not be my blessing or my curse:
The illusion's gone for ever, and thou art
    Insensible, I trust, but none the worse,
And in thy stead I've got a deal of judgment,
Though heaven knows how it ever found a lodgment.

                [Canto I, stanzas 214, 215]

I quoted though, I am sure, without seeing any relevance to what I was making of, getting out of, Job.

Such lessons can take a long time to learn. Some thirty years later, having to lecture on Job in the then new general education program at Harvard, I was still—so such notes as I retain seem to show—offering an audience of about a thousand a reading of Job not so very unlike the one I spoke for among my Adult School students. And now—another thirty years on—what do I find now to say of these pages?

Let me begin by describing the Book of Job as a type specimen, a means of examining and displaying some highly general and important features of a reader's situation. It is a type specimen. in these respects.

(1) Being a *first order* thing: the most challenging of all occasions for reflecting on what such rankings derive from.

(2) Being extremely *remote* from me: remote in all sorts of ways and for many reasons. As a creation of quite different minds from mine, minds that lived in and were shaped by quite different conditions—linguistic, social, cultural, intellectual, moral—

The Book of Job

Job calls for a venture in imaginative penetration and construction by the reader that will, I think, seem the more demanding the more we reflect upon it. But indeed, were we to reflect upon it enough (to use so questionable a term), we might decide that the venture is too marvelous, too wonderful for us and give up—*give up* in a fashion not much unlike that in which Job himself gives up (42:3, 5, 6) at the end of his colloquy with God.

Such remotenesses are, of course, in some measure relevant to all reading; Job just illustrates them in the extremest degree. Any literature springing from and dealing with situations differing widely from a reader's must raise these problems, whether it is the *Iliad* he has opened or the latest portrayal of an urban ghetto. I use the word *relevant* here because it has been a catchword of so much recent protest and revolt against studies which do not, immediately and obviously, fit (and spring from) the supposed situation and needs of the reader. Some of this protest is, no doubt, reasonable and intelligent. Some is not. The problem is: What is the reader's situation? And what are the needs springing from it? To consider these questions reflectively is to realize that *relevant* and *remote* are related words with by no means simple meanings. Job presents an extraordinarily testing opportunity for exploring and appraising their implications.

Certainly they are not, on most occasions, direct opposites, though they can be so used. (For many situations what is most relevant can be vastly remote. And it may well be the very fact that it is remote that makes it relevant.) We have, moreover, to distinguish remoteness as removal in time, circumstance, and in other describable respects from consciously felt incompatibilities, less easy to describe. T. S. Eliot once wrote to me that reading any remote author is like trying to be on both sides of a mirror at once.

To come back, however, to Job. It serves me here as type specimen of the radically great and of the radically remote and in three other ways.

(3) Being in grave disorder and needing therefore hazardous reconstruction.

(4) Being highly manifold in meanings.

(5) Being indeterminate.

These respects are connected and I will be taking them together. Much of what follows will be exemplification of this connectedness.

No one can acquire even a slight acquaintance with the history of scholarly opinion on the Book of Job (the outer testimony) without learning how many and how diverse have been the ways in which it has been taken: both as a whole and in parts, single verses, and key words. There is hardly any question which can be—reasonably or unreasonably—raised about the book which has not been answered by able people in irreconcilable ways. It is not alone in this among Sacred Books, of course, but it may well be the extremest instance. A reading of Robert Pfeiffer's chapter in his *Introduction to the Old Testament* [1] (one of the great unlocking books of our time) or a comparison of a few translations—the Authorized with the Revised versions, the Anchor with the New English and with William Baron Stevenson's 1946 rendering, *The Poem of Job*—will show how differently the most qualified scholars can take it; and how open, how *indeterminate* the best of them are ready to leave many of its problems.

To begin with the biggest of these. What appears in the Bible as the Book of Job consists of a prose prelude and a prose epilogue, with, sandwiched in between them, a poetic drama in formal verse. So much is now agreed upon. What is uncertain, and not becoming any clearer, is the relation between the folktale frame—the narrative opening and end—and the poem. How the poem came to be so framed and when, what the frame does to it, and myriad derivative minor questions still admit of great differences of opinion. As a result the import of the book as a whole and of the poem, if it is taken separately, remains indeterminate. I shall be trying to show what this indeterminateness can do for a reader.

1. (New York: Harper, 1948).

The Book of Job

The prose opening and the prose end are folk tale at its highest but with a calculatedly enigmatic character for the opening, which is focused in the baffling figure of Satan (the Adversary), a figure associated with prodigious consequences for our tradition. Folk-tale opening and folk-tale end are, *as they stand,* shaped to presuppose and require some sort of colloquy between Job and his three friends (the 'comforters') who come to visit him. The verse drama appears, superficially, to supply this. But just before it begins comes a brief prose transition and immediately after its close another prose transition dealing with the three friends and disposing of them. It is these two junction pieces that stick the prose tale and the verse drama together. The big problem, *What, if anything, have the tale and the poem to do with one another?,* naturally turns in part on these short transitional passages. They need to be pondered in close connection with what precedes and follows them in the tale as well as with what may be thought to take place in the drama. There are also a number of breaks in the poem—matter of varying quality, some great and some mediocre, having been inserted; and there is evidence of considerable disturbance—some speeches being out of order and some probably missing. (See table, page 46.)

I will continue with the big, over-all contrasts, postponing discussion of the transitions as well as of the epilogue (42:10–17)—the turning of "the captivity of Job" and the restoration of his fortunes—until the prologue (1–2:13) has been minutely examined.

In setting out these contrasts we have first to realize that what must, to a careful examination, seem to be inconsistencies—disaccords, failures in plausibility of all degrees and sorts—have not been, in general, seen as such by a majority of traditional readers. Most of these have taken smoothly and without question much that seems surprising, even inexplicable, to the modern student. Whoever first put the folk tale and the poem together presumably felt that each would sufficiently support the other.

Beyond

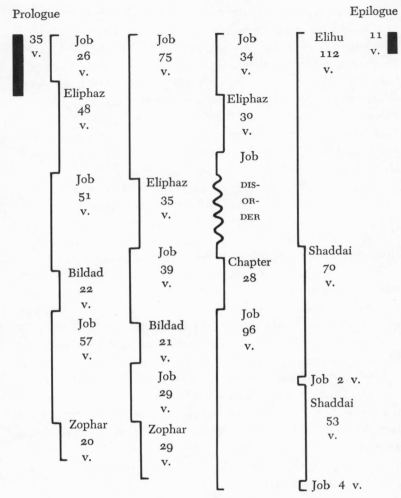

Prologue 35 v.

Epilogue 11 v.

Job 26 v.

Eliphaz 48 v.

Job 51 v.

Bildad 22 v.

Job 57 v.

Zophar 20 v.

Job 75 v.

Eliphaz 35 v.

Job 39 v.

Bildad 21 v.

Job 29 v.

Zophar 29 v.

Job 34 v.

Eliphaz 30 v.

Job DIS-OR-DER

Chapter 28

Job 96 v.

Elihu 112 v.

Shaddai 70 v.

Job 2 v.

Shaddai 53 v.

Job 4 v.

Approximate lengths of parts of Job

And, indeed, he was right—as is proved by the career which this strangely ill-accordant collocation has had. This is a fact with which our doubts and questionings and complaints must deal, however disturbing we may find it. Indisputably, many trained, intent, and able specialists have not been in the least troubled by discrepancies in the design that seem glaringly obvious to others. As Pfeiffer's review of the history of critical judgment shows, the variety of opinion on the book's integrity, date, and provenance is daunting. On the key issue, his summary is: "The critics have suggested every possibility: the prologue, the epilogue, or both (in part or *in toto*), were written by the author of the poem, or before him, or after him. . . . The evidence is not conclusive." [2] Nonetheless, all this has to be balanced by the book's generally unembarrassed acceptance through the ages by less scholarly readers.

The account which follows adopts what W. B. Stevenson lays down as "the fundamental principle that in the first place the poem should be studied by itself apart." [3] So studied, the following facts about it are to be remarked.

(1) Job's afflictions, as they are precisely specified in the tale, are (a) loss of all his property and cattle and flocks and servants (except four, who survived to tell him each his tale) and of his children, and (b) loathsome sores. The poem makes no mention of either (a) or (b). Instead, in a somewhat indefinite fashion, it presents Job as having been pulled down from high status, power, and honor to utter ruin, scorn, and loss of friends; to jeopardy and perhaps actual physical maltreatment through conspiracy by opponents, thriving malefactors—the Miscreants, as Stevenson calls them—who are prospering in part through having overthrown Job. This other set of calamities gives, I think, the poem far wider and deeper means of arraigning the governance of affairs than the peculiarly special occasion the tale provides. For the poem, these same Miscreants, who have taken advantage of Job's very virtues to undo him, are Shaddai's (a name replacing *Jahveh*) chosen and favored agents. What they do to honest, noble-minded, decent, "God-fearing," charitable, and helpful people becomes, for Job, Shaddai's will. Job's agony of resentment passes beyond his own molesters to the Power which has, regardlessly, allowed them—indeed, almost patently encouraged them—to mistreat him despite (or because of) his virtues. This

2. Ibid., pp. 667–78.
3. In the preface to his *The Poem of Job* (London: Oxford, 1948).

profoundly moral and religious issue is the theme of the poem: something far more momentous than the mere breaking down "without cause" of a "God-fearing" man and his patching up, equally causeless, that the tale recounts. The wrong the poem studies is something that could not possibly be so lightly, so heartlessly, so irresponsibly, so imperceptively 'righted'. But in how many ways the problems that the poem of Job faces transcend any that the Old Testament—apart from a few verses in the prophets—can conceive of!

(2) In the poem Job has an active quarrel with Shaddai. In the tale the very spring of the action is that by nothing that is done to him can he be brought to complain. The Job of the poem is as bitterly in revolt as the Job of the tale is unquestioningly supine and superlatively submissive. It is hard to imagine greater contrast.

(3) The poem knows nothing of Satan, the Adversary, or of what—for the tale—is, by Jahveh's will, the prime source of Job's afflictions. In a debate between the friends and Job—none of whom is informed of any of this—such omission is no problem. But when the action moves over to become an exchange between Job and Shaddai, some reference or echo, however indirect, might well be expected. But, indeed, the contrast in character between the Jahveh of the tale and the El or Eloah or Shaddai of the poem is as great even as that between the two Jobs. Jahveh has a court over which he presides as a judge deeply and personally concerned with human conduct and what it should be. But Shaddai is a terrific architectonic energy, violently presenting himself as unimaginable, and exulting in his very incomprehensibility and lack of concern for man.

The scene for the poem cannot be that described in Chapter 2 (12–13). This Job of the poem is *not* sitting on the town dump, as in the tale, banished there because of his physical noisomeness. And the friends have *not*, in the poem, "rent every one his mantle, and sprinkled dust upon their heads toward heaven" (2:12), whether to express grief on Job's account or, as unsympathetic commentators have suggested, to ward off the danger

of becoming infected themselves by the curse that has evidently
fallen on Job. (Those friends of the tale are friends indeed!) No.
The setting of the poem is one in which Job can say: "My bed
shall comfort me, my couch shall ease my complaint" (7:13),
and then (Stevenson's translation): "If I say 'my bed will comfort me, my couch will carry my sorrows'" (7:13). "Then in
dreams you [Shaddai] terrorize me and with visions you engulf
me" (7:14). "And you choose to choke my life, to let me suffer
rather than die" (7:15). He has a bed, though it does him little
good. Stevenson, combining many indications, makes out a case
that the Job of the poem is actually in some sort of confinement,
in the power of his enemies; so that when he says to his friends:

> Such you have not become to me;
>   you see my calamity, and are afraid.
> Have I said, "Make me a gift"?
>   Or, "From your wealth offer a bribe for me"?
> Or, "Deliver me from the adversary's hand"?
>   Or, "Ransom me from the hand of oppressors"?

what is referred to would be a real ransom he might have asked
for but did not. Similarly (7:12):

> Am I a sea, or a sea monster
> That thou settest a watch over me?

This, which is addressed to Shaddai, as in the end responsible,
would refer to real guards. Job's enemies, the Miscreants of the
poem, are Shaddai's agents, active with his permission as much
as Satan in the tale is doing the Lord's will. The Job of the tale
knew nothing of Satan. The Job of the poem knows all about his
very different overthrowers, and that Shaddai supports them is
his premise. So, too, at the very end of the play, Shaddai's last
words, "that your own right hand give you victory" (40:14),
would be about those who, on Shaddai's behalf, hold Job in their
power. Nothing, however, anywhere indicates that the friends
have grounds to fear these Miscreants. They are visitors from
other countries. A possible stage setting for the drama could
therefore be a prison, and relevant parallels could be with

Beyond

Socrates, condemned to death for obeying Apollo, or with *The Consolation of Philosophy*. Boethius, however, while awaiting execution, was won over by the comforting offered to him. Job was not.

That two compositions so opposed in so many respects have been so readily accepted as forming a consistent work is, I think, deeply instructive. And these contrasts grow the more interesting the more closely we examine what have been called above the transition passages in their contexts and as related to the prologue, to which we will now turn.

Let us review in detail the familiar opening. That Job was "blameless and upright" is affirmed at the start, stated axiomatically in the first verse. The prologue is ostensibly a recounting of the testing of his merit and the verse drama is a debate upon it. That it has been thus put beyond doubt is therefore important. And the epilogue, in its folk-tale way, confirms this fully. Job is also "the greatest of all the children of the east" (1:3), and the tale suggests that this outstanding position is an immediate consequence (Deuteronomic fashion) of his virtue. Moreover, the Lord (of the folk tale, who is there called Jahveh, whereas the poem uses *El* thirty-six times, *Eloah* thirty-five times, *Shaddai* twenty-five times, and *Jahveh* never, the superscriptions to 38:1, 40:1–3, 6, and 42:1 not being from the poet) expressly and publicly states that Job is "blameless," adding "that there is none like him in the earth." A notable admission, this, confirming the axiomatic character of the first verse. It is as though the tale were inviting us to witness an experimental demonstration relevant to a theorem (as of the properties of a perfect gas).

The character of this Lord of the folk tale is not quite as evident as it is sometimes taken to be. It afforded no less a student of character than Jung—in his *Answer to Job*—much deep enjoyment and, maybe, more bafflement than he admits. His ostensible fun with this deity—who neglects so often to avail himself of his omniscience—and the arresting, indeed paralyzing, drama Jung concocts as the outcome of the blundering may lead us to take too simple a view. But no reflective view of any deity can be truly simple. It is certainly too easy to say that the Lord here is just a stock or typical Oriental potentate; a blown-up sheik or Solomon, with his court in due attendance, and rather pompously proud of his dutiful servant and prize subject, Job. Fearsome though that presentation would be, suggesting a grim view of life for the taleteller and his audience, to allow Jahveh a more continuous omniscience would yield something more daunting still, something perhaps that would explain why Job, in verse 5, should rise so early to burn so many offerings. Part of his perfect piety in the folk tale is that he "feared God"—though that should not be taken to be the whole reason why "he eschewed evil." His perfect fear of God could well lead him to suspect his sons. He would understand why they might "have sinned and cursed God in their hearts." Was their sin just that cursing? Or was the cursing the outcome of other sin and of the conviction that God would surely know about it and in due course requite them? Whichever way we read it, the probability of this Lord's knowledge of their hearts (and of Job's own heart, too) is strongly implied. That knowledge is, I think, almost required if Job's fear is to be perfect. What is done to him in the rest of the tale is enough, we may think, to show that his fear was fully justified. To allow omniscience is, moreover, to put the Lord's exchanges with Satan in an even stranger light. Jung may laugh, though sardonically. But if we take Jahveh to have a Miltonic omniscience, we may rather find reason to tremble.

The sons of God (1:6), their relation to Satan, and the nature of this ceremonial occasion are not matters on which information can be found elsewhere.[4] The taleteller's stature is shown by the uncanny power he has of making his few sentences convey so much and stir such conjectures.

Clearly it was not usual for Satan to attend these functions.

4. The poem supplies little or nothing to help us with them, though the shouting for joy when the cornerstone of the foundations of the earth was laid (38:7) is one of the few indications that the author of the poem may possibly have read or heard the tale.

Beyond

Whether he, too, was one of the sons of God (Jung suggests that he was the eldest of them, and may have good grounds), he was not, at least overtly,[5] expected. "Whence cometh thou?" (1:6) and Satan's reply (1:7) prepare for the citation of Job (1:8).

Assuming the Lord's omniscience, Job is not being tested; he is instead being used in an operation on Satan. Satan's undermining question "Doth Job fear God for nought?" puts in doubt *everything*: not only Job's morality, scaling down his being ?blameless and upright? to being ᵛshrewd, realistic, and politicˢʷ. He is, Satan suggests, merely keeping up his side of a mutual-benefit understanding with the Lord, a suggestion that could be wounding and angering. We may imagine, if we like, a sizable generation gap between the Lord and Satan.

If this understanding is broken by the Lord, Job will respond by breaking his side of it, too (1:11). That is Satan's position. And it is to show him that he is mistaken that the Lord authorizes him, and virtually directs him, to perform upon Job the merciless experiments of the tale.[6] As the other uses of the word translated by "renounce" or "blaspheme" or "curse" show (in 1:5 and 2:9 especially), the renouncing would amount to giving up the game. Job's wife (for whose share in Job's suffering—they are her children, too—the taleteller has, we may think, a marked disregard) is certain that the immediate consequence of the

5. It is noteworthy that the supposal of the Lord's omniscience—here as elsewhere—adds singular import to actions, as with this question in which he pretends not to know.

6. It may be helpful to compare Seton Pollock's deeply pondered account: "A prose introduction sets the stage . . . and tells of an altercation between God and an Angelic Being in heaven. . . . [This] makes the emphasis clear, and represents Job as being unaware that he was being used to vindicate an eternal truth.

The matter to be settled was whether a good man is good because it pays . . . or whether goodness will remain when every material incentive to goodness has been swept away," *Stubborn Soil* (London: Sidgwick, 1946). The resemblance of this to the problem posed in Book II of the *Republic* will be noted. Whether "altercation" really fits the heavenly exchanges seems doubtful and equally whether the means used in this "vindication" of "truth" can in any way whatever be justified.

renouncing would be Job's death. Again, though, we must note what the Lord's omniscience would do to the story. If omniscient, he knows that Job will not, in fact, either curse God or "charge God with foolishness" (1:22)—a phrase variously translated as "foolishly charge God" or "ascribe aught unseemly to God."

The use of this phrase shows how capable the taleteller and his audiences were of audacity in conjecture. Everything about Satan is further proof. In his two speeches (1:9–11 and 2:4, 5) he flatly offers the Lord instruction. It might be that he does not quite know yet to Whom he is talking. That the Lord already knows the outcome (and presumably has already made it such that it will refute his agent's prediction) has not occurred to Satan. What the effect of the refutation upon him is, we are not told. We can, though, imagine him reflecting more deeply on the formidable nature of a being capable of accepting his proposals and of giving him the power to put them into effect. Nonetheless, he again offers the Lord advice (2:5).

It is to be noted that Satan required the Lord's permission. He acts as the Lord's agent and executive. The source of Job's afflictions is the Lord himself—though it has taken Satan's theorizing (tauntingly and irritatingly displayed) to bring such action forth. That it is all really the Lord's doing much enhances the significance of the action. And this whether or not we stress as much as I have above the component of his foreknowledge, an aspect that can be separated only by artifice from his omnipotence.[7]

Supposing full foreknowledge, what does the action do (a) for Job, (b) for Satan, (c) for the Lord?

(a) For Job it confirms and deepens the conviction which has been the ground of his fear throughout. He puts it in final fashion in his reply to his wife (2:10). The Lord, he now knows to the uttermost, can apportion evil as well as good; and this not

7. That the Lord knows what will happen because—before Time was—he ordained that it should be so, puts the two aspects into intelligible connection.

for the recipient's correction or other benefit, but sheerly and for no reason whatever that is within range of the victim's surmises. At best, this fearful and fear-confirming knowledge can strengthen in him what has been throughout a principle of prudence. It can increase his care to give no excuse, no handle of any sort, for further affliction. He has to be as blameless as ever. We will be considering below what may be our interpretations of the remainder of 2:10—"In all this did not Job sin with his lips," and especially of these last three words.

(b) For Satan this refutation of his theories of human motives may be thought to have destroyed him. He disappears; he is not heard from or of again. It is plain that his role in this action is not that of any other figure in literature—whether called by his name or not. He is neither the originator of evil—the first of the fallen—nor the Tempter. Nor, if we allow the Lord his omniscience, will Satan be the Celestial Head of Intelligence Services, chief of the FBI, the super spy, as Tur Sinai and Marvin H. Pope (in *Job*, vol. 15 of the Anchor Bible) suppose him to have been. He is not in the least the Lord's opponent or rival—except as having held a view of Job contrary to that of the Lord. This view has now been disposed of by demonstration and with it goes some considerable part of Satan. Not all of him, however. He has been wrong about Job, but he may be right about all other men. Did not the Lord himself affirm of Job that "there is none like him in the earth" (1:8): the statement that made this psychologist, Satan, speak out. There is possibly no other character who establishes himself so solidly with so few words. His mocking, repetitive answer to the Lord's reiterative question, "Whence cometh thou?"—"From going to and fro in the earth and walking up and down in it"—when he has just been doing, as the Lord knows, so much more, gives him extraordinary stature. (Are all his goings and walkings of this nature?) The Lord, however, contrives to outdo him in irony—also through repetition: "Hast thou considered my servant Job?" In view of what Satan must be thinking of Job, of his own failure despite the terrible treatment he has been directed to administer, and—

should we not add?—his new perception of the character of the Lord as it is now being revealed, these exchanges are hard indeed to match in all literature.

The end of 2:3, "to destroy him [to swallow him up] without cause," supports the view that Job's wife would be right in equating "curse God" and "die." Job did not yield; if he had, that would have been the end of him. Such seems the implication. But "without cause" remains highly significant. Since he did not yield, there has been no cause for, nothing to justify, what has been done to him: an admission that troubles neither Satan nor the Lord in the least, as they ruthlessly proceed to the next round of torture.

(c) Let us leave to Jung the problem of what these experiments do for the Lord. Satan's phrasing (2:4) in proposing the next atrocity invites consideration: "Skin within skin. All that a man has will he give for his life." The skin is relatively superficial. So are a man's mere possessions. The expression may be proverbial. By letting all go, a man may save his skin. The contrast is with "his bone and his flesh." The Lord's consent is as smooth as before: "Behold, he is in thine hand." The addition "only spare his life" is partly an echo of Satan's "All that a man has he will give for his life." Partly it is a reminder (diamond against diamond) to Satan that he must not, by accident *or design*, spoil the experiment. If Job were to be slain, we would not learn whether he would have cursed God to his face or not. Anyone with the grim taste for such experiments that Satan and the Lord share might wish to know what would have happened had they offered Job the option of *saving his life* by cursing God, the being about whom he now knows, perhaps, more. May some dramatist soon show us this. One is tempted to speculate further. What would be the outcome of Job's learning (say from Satan or—Quixote-wise—from a copy of the folk tale of Job brought him by a friend) just why he has been thus afflicted? Would it be correct for him still—even then—to refrain from protest in thought as well as in utterance? Would that still be to "hold fast thine integrity," as Dinah puts it, his simple, undivided wholeness of

Beyond

being? Or is there a further, a more entire integrity which would decline to connive at being so treated? Satan's repeated phrase "curse thee *to thy face*" links up with the last three words of this prelude, "with his lips" (2:10). "To thy face" contrasts with "behind thy back," as "with his lips" contrasts with "in his heart." Both evidently raise again the question of the Lord's omniscience. Both take us back to 1:5: Why did Job offer so many sacrifices? "Thus did Job continually."

More than a little of the power of the prologue may derive from these uncertainties. And calling it a folk tale could badly misrepresent it. There is a folk tale that has been found in many lands in varying forms with the same general plot. This prose prelude, however, is a very finely worked version, using to the utmost repetitions which can be understood in subtly different ways as they return. The narrator's art in not closing alternatives out and in leaving possibilities open is something from which his exegetes can certainly learn important lessons. We have been watching throughout this review how the questions these equivocal phrases raise lead us to other phrases which raise again the same unresolved questions. If we step now from "with his lips" (2:10) to a poem expanding on this theme, it will be to observe there again the same pattern of open alternatives. To state some of these may help. One view is that Job *was* sinning deeply in his heart, blaspheming there vigorously, managing to control his tongue, and uttering only the blameless words which have ever since been of so much exalted service.

This view can look to the opening of Psalm 39:

> I said, I will take heed to my ways:
> That I sin not with my tongue.
> I will keep my mouth with a bridle,
> While the wicked is in sight.

It would be extravagant, no doubt, to read "the wicked" here as referring to Jahveh, however much the author of *Milton's God* may think we should do so. The label has too much use in the Psalms, in opposition to the pious or righteous, for any such interpretation to be acceptable. But if Job were secretly blaspheming, he had reason enough to go the whole way.

Another view is that all such notions are themselves blasphemous and that Job—being blameless and upright, axiomatically or by definition—is still holding fast his integrity in his undivided heart, too, whatever the foolish may find to say. This view may also appeal to Psalm 39, which has an odd way of repeatedly seeming relevant either to the tale or to the poem of Job:

> I was dumb, I opened not my mouth;
> Because thou didst it.

A third view is that "with his lips" is to be taken as a deliberately contrived ambiguity introduced by whoever fitted the poem into its prose frame. Its aim would then be to make more consonant the passages of the poem in which Job is the very reverse of acquiescent, far indeed from being dumb; being, in fact, truly aflame with protest, expostulation, and challenge. This also can quote the same Psalm (39:3):

> My heart was hot within me
> While I was musing the fire kindled:
> Then spake I with my tongue.

The three uncommonly devoted friends are said—in additions to the LXX translation of Job, drawn from a folk tale—to have come from afar and to have been kings, as Job was. What they find is a Job so changed that they do not know him. Their ritual recognition of their grief—rending their robes and sprinkling dust upon their heads—is similar to that with which Job had greeted his initial disasters. After that they sit with him on that haunting village dunghill seven days and seven nights in silence. It is this silence which is broken by Job's opening words of the poem: "Let the day perish wherein I was born." (May there be no more that day among the round of them, since it did this.)

No contrast can outdo that between the storm of imprecation which follows (only outdone in violence by the Voice out of the whirlwind which at the end answers) and the acquiescence in which Job has last spoken: "What? Shall we receive good at the hand of God, and shall we not receive evil?"

Occasion to wonder anew at the innumerable readers who have been able, calmly content, to take such unexceedable irreconciliabilities in their stride.

3

Job: Poem and Epilogue

It may help perspective here if we compare two utterances from other springs and headwaters of our culture which, in their opposed ways, present answers to the closing questions (Job 2:10) of the prologue. One is from the *Iliad*, from Achilles' first speech to Priam when the old king visits him to ransom Hector's body (XXIV, 527–533):

The gods have spun the thread for us this way—to live in pain, all we who die—but they themselves are without sorrow. Two urns stand on the floor of Zeus and in one are good gifts and in the other evil. And the man for whom Zeus, Lord of the thunder, mixes the gifts he sends, that man will meet now with evil, now with good; but the man to whom he gives only his evil gifts must journey over the face of the sacred earth unhonored either by gods or men.[1]

Job, receiving unmixed evil in place of the former unmixed good, becomes similarly unhonored. With this compare Plato on these very lines (379D):

1. From I. A. Richards' version of the *Iliad*, *The Wrath of Achilles* (New York: Norton, 1950).

59

Beyond

Socrates: That which is good is not the cause of all things, but only of things which are as it is right for them to be. Then that which is good is not responsible for the coming into being of evil.

Adeimantus: Right.

Socrates: If that be so, then God, inasmuch as he is good, is not the cause of all things, as the common belief goes. . . . And though the good things come from no other than God, the causes of the ill things are in something other, not in him.

Adeimantus: That seems to be most true.

Socrates: Then away with all the sayings in Homer that God gives good *and* evil chances.[2]

Three diverse springs indeed—Homer, Plato, and the prose prelude; they are confluents to a tradition within which, *as yet,* means of distinguishing and analyzing what they contribute remain strangely little developed, less still the means of relating and reconciling them. To these three the poem of Job brings in a fourth set of attitudes and conjectures certainly as different from that of the prologue as Plato is from Homer. Moreover, it should be noted that *within* each of these confluents, as *between* them, different and opposing positions are not only present but *active,* thereby sustaining tensions without which their hold and sway in our tradition would be far slighter. We have been considering some of the tensions constituting the prologue, building up its peculiar force. Those *within* the poem of Job are not a whit less essential; nor are those *between* it and the tale. But the poem, furthermore, contrasts with all three—Homer, prologue, and *Republic*—in developing a diversity and intensity of dramatic action which makes them seem relatively simple. This, however, risks underrating the background tension of the *Republic,* which comes to the forefront only in its final pages with the myth of Er. In any case *Iliad*:*Republic*::tale:poem. Some sort of opposition, of ratio, proportion, or analogy, is asking here for clarification. Before proceeding to the dramatic structure of the poem, it may be well to try to bring some key meanings of ᵂoppose ᵂ into sharper focus.

2. From I. A. Richards' *Plato's Republic* (London: Cambridge, 1966).

Job: Poem and Epilogue

Despite their negative appearance and seeming reliance on the contradictory and the contrary, the positive force of these relations is evident. Without the opposition of ^{sw}there^{sw}, ^{sw}here^{sw} would lapse. And, reciprocally, ^{sw}there^{sw} requires ^{sw}here^{sw}. Similarly for ^{sw}this^{sw} and ^{sw}that^{sw}. So, too, for ^{sw}now^{sw} and ^{sw}then^{sw}, but with the differences due to the linear structure of time as opposed to the three dimensions of space. In these, each term ^{nb}requires^{nb} its opposite—in a sense that can probably not be indicated without (or better than through) these instances. They are fundamental as setting up the framework for perception of space and time; but more fundamental still, perhaps, as supplying the means of apprehending this sense of 'requires', and, with that, gaining insight into the positive force of opposition.

What other instances can we find of the work of this high-ranking universal (this constitutive form, this classifying label, this indispensible instrument of thought), this intelligential toolmaker's tool?[3] We have been reminded by such tools (as well as

3. On the significance of the toolmaking tool for the emergence of the "solely human achievements," the following comparisons will repay pondering:

"The ultimate phylogenetic question of linguistics, the origin of language, has been proscribed by the neogrammarian tenet, but at present the emergence of language must be brought together with the other changes which mark the transition from prehuman to human society. Such a juxtaposition can also give certain clues for a relative chronology. Thus, attempts have been made to elucidate the genetic interrelation between language and visual art. Figurative art seems to imply the presence of language and thus the earliest vestiges of representative art provide glottogony with a plausible *terminus ante quem*.

"Moreover, we may connect three universals among the solely human achievements: (1) manufacture of tools to build tools; (2) rise of phonemic, purely distinctive elements, deprived of their own meaning but used to build meaningful units, namely morphemes and words; (3) incest taboo, conclusively interpreted by anthropologists as the indispensable precondition for a wider exchange of mates and thereby for an expansion of kinship and for a consequent buildup of economic, cooperative, and defensive alliances. In brief, this device serves to create men's 'solidarity transcending the family.' As a matter of fact, all of these three innovations introduce pure auxiliaries, secondary tools necessary for the foundation of human society with its material, verbal, and spiritual culture. An abstract mediate principle lies in the idea of secondary tools, and the emergence of all of

served by them all through) in our attempts to apprehend what the first two chapters of Job put before us.

The most instructive of these instances may be that of the opposition between any power and its limits. This is most strikingly illustrated by omnipotence and its derivative omniscience which made their problematic and fluctuant appearance in the previous chapter. Do we not have to admit that if we annul, drop, occult the necessary limit, the power vanishes too? Nothing can be done unless something *cannot* be done; nothing be known unless something *cannot* be known. Even minimal exploration of the extent of a power becomes nugatory if the power is supposed to be *un*limited. This is not to deny the possibility of great powers, far exceeding any familiar to us or readily imaginable. But we will probably be wise if we posit that these boundary determinations, such as were active in our discussion of Jahveh's omniscience, are matters rather of dramatic appropriateness, rhetorical positioning [4] under the safe-conduct of literary tact, than of directly logical, philosophical, or moral decisions. Tact in interpretation here is, in fact, deputizing for such decisions past and to come.

This proposal itself—what these last pages have been trying to put forward—is a set of positings [5] exhibited not with the aim

---

their three aspects must have been the cardinal step from 'animality' toward the thoroughly human mind. The rudiments of these three fundamentally similar possessions must have emerged within the same paleontological period, and the earliest excavated specimens of tools—such as gravers or burins—destined to make tools enable us to posit a conjectural glottogonic epoch," Roman Jakobson, in *Main Trends of Research in the Social and Human Sciences* (Paris: Mouton, 1970), pp. 444–45. The four final paragraphs of this amazingly wide-ranging survey will be found particularly relevant to the topics I am here exploring.

4. What may seem obscure or dismissive here may perhaps become a little better lighted and more committed if these remarks are compared with those ventured in "Final Landing Stage" in my *Interpretation in Teaching;* and in "Reorientation" in my *Poetries and Sciences* (New York: Norton, 1970).

5. It is not easy to find a richer field of vital interconnections, a more important ganglion in our language, than the system represented by the

of asserting truths or advancing views or persuading, but rather (= ᴰearlier, soonerᴰ) of inviting certain sorts of experimentation with them, pre-eminently—in highly momentous matters, those typically with which the Book of Job is concerned—the trying out of a number of probably irreconcilable possibilities as worth co-entertainment. The model, or type specimen, is in what has been done, with such world-transforming success, in physics, the necessary stance for which has been discussed, since Niels Bohr, under the heading of Complementarity. In comparison with which, traditional and current practice in the humanities seems to have been sadly mistaken. The assumption that one should "make up one's mind" about meanings—as one can make up a bed with a view to sleeping in it—may be needlessly frustrating and wasteful.

From this, which is far from being an excursion, we may now turn to the second transitional passage in Job, the junction piece (42:7–10) between the poem and the epilogue. We will find that it raises further doubts about the compatibility of the enclosed poem with its frame.

The chief discomforts it causes, the principal misfits, are (1) that the poem ends with Job speaking, but the prose frame continues (42:7):

And it was so, that after the LORD had spoken these words unto Job, the LORD said . . .

So we have to try to guess which words this Lord had been speaking. This is awkward enough and suggests that something has gone wrong. But (2) what the Lord says to Eliphaz the Temanite is (42:7):

---

related entries PAUSE, POSE, POSSE, POSSESS in Eric Partridge's *Origins*. They can be compared with the semantically (in part) parallel system of uses of *put*. After a reflective perusal of these, the positing of an essential dependency of being upon opposition looks immemorial, both as condition for coming to be and as earliest insight. It is no accident that the system includes *poser* and *puzzle*. There are times when—without warning us—the choreography of the etymons seems to have long ago settled our fundamental procedures for us.

Beyond

My wrath is kindled against thee, and against thy two friends: for ye
have not spoken of me the thing that is right, as my servant Job hath.

This plainly requires us to look carefully at what the three friends
have said, at what Job has said, and, most carefully of all, at
what Shaddai has said in the poem. We should especially note
that here in this junction passage to the epilogue, Jahveh again
(not Shaddai) is speaking. He is plainly the same Jahveh of the
prologue, using again his phrase "my servant Job," for which the
poem has no use whatever. These two, Jahveh and Shaddai, are,
perhaps necessarily, as different as the two Jobs with whom they
are concerned. As the worshiper so the worshiped.[6] The Job who
rose up early (1:5) requires a fearsome, suspicious FBI-type
Jahveh. The unquenchably protesting Job of the poem calls for
an unceremonious cosmic force in the thunderstorm to answer
him. This may seem an extreme means of pointing up their difference. But commentaries on Job supply endless instances of
obstinate blurring. The two concepts of these deities are not the
same. To call them by the same name is an invitation to identify
them: to mistake, yet again, ways of conceiving ꞌXꞌ for ꞌXꞌ itself.
Too often in Biblical and theological studies the term *God* is no
better than a verbal smoke screen. A huge semantic problem, of
course, arises here—as daunting in its way as the Voice from the
whirlwind. W. B. Stevenson (in *The Poem of Job*), for example,
remarks about ʷShaddaiʷ that it "is to be understood by English
readers as an exact synonym for God." We know, of course, that
he is merely referring us to the Dictionary. But still, in a discussion of verbal uses in such a source as Job, how obfuscating a
procedure!

We have in the prologue two examples of "the thing that is
right" as spoken of Jahveh by Job. They are among the most
famous and familiar verses in the Bible (Job 1:21 and 2:10):

6. How widely this correspondence may be observed is probably best left
an empirical matter. If we make it a *principle*, a necessary correlation, we
will very likely have turned it by definition into no more than an empty
truism: a man's ideas accord with the man. It seems much more than that.

and he said, Naked came I out of my mother's womb, and naked shall I return thither: the LORD gave, and the LORD hath taken away; blessed be the name of the LORD.

But he said unto her, Thou speakest as one of the foolish women speaketh. What? shall we receive good at the hand of God, and shall we not receive evil? In all this did not Job sin with his lips.

It is by comparison with these that we have to judge whether Jahveh in 42:7 can possibly be referring to speeches made by Job and by the three friends in the poem. The conclusion to which these comparisons should lead, if normal standards of interpretation are in control, is that Jahveh in 42:7 is talking about speeches very different indeed from those of the poem. As we have seen, one of the subsidiary interests of the study of the Book of Job is the degree to which devotional and other factors can influence interpretation and put otherwise decisive evidence out of focus.

Stevenson has, except on one highly important point, well summarized what the evidence as a whole allows as conjecture on the tale-poem relation. The poet—inheriting the theme of injured and suffering goodness and the problem of divine justice it raises—may have created the characters of Job and his three friends. If so, the tale may have been in part a derivative from the poem originating in some purely Jewish circle. But the tale may have existed before the poem, which borrowed the name and known character of Job and conceivably those of the three friends. If so, the debt of the poem to the tale is, Stevenson concludes, "very small." The poem "has drastically altered the behaviour and the final fortune" of Job. In the poem "he is a convinced and determined rebel, who receives no vindication and is not delivered from his distress." In the tale "he bears his trials with unbroken patience and receives the due reward of his goodness. The poet leaves Job reconciled to his fate but still a sufferer, quite distinct from the vigorous, prosperous and happy Job of the folk-tale." We may doubt, I think, whether the

Beyond

Job of the poem is truly "reconciled to his fate." All that he says at the end in response to (40:2):

> Is the case against Shaddai abandoned?
> Will God's accuser continue?

is (I use Stevenson's translation of 40:4):

I am too petty to make reply. I place my hand upon my mouth; I have spoken once. I will not repeat, twice (indeed). I will not say more.

This, which may not be without its ironical ingredients, earns him (40:7-14) a further cloudburst of sarcastic questions and wounding mockery. His reply in the final verses of Chapter 42 has seemed to many different readers—stretching their powers of comprehending to the utmost—to have extraordinarily different possible significances. Whether they show Job as "reconciled to his fate" is, surely, a most searching question, able to make us reconsider our concepts of reconciliation.

I quote both the Revised Version:

1 Then Job answered, and said
2 I know that thou canst do all things,
  And that no purpose of thine can be restrained.
3 "Who is this that hideth counsel without knowledge?"
  Therefore have I uttered that which I understood not,
  Things too wonderful for me, which I knew not.

. . . .

5 I had heard of thee by the hearing of the ear;
  But now mine eye seeth thee.
6 Wherefore I abhor myself, and repent
  In dust and ashes.

and Stevenson's translation:

I grant you to be all powerful, no design is beyond your reach,
I admit to have argued rashly of wonders beyond my ken,
I had heard by hearsay of you but now my eyes have seen you.
I, therefore, retreat entirely. I repent over earth and ashes.

66

Job: Poem and Epilogue

Here, 3a can be taken as an echo of Shaddai's first shattering question. But verse 4 seems clearly to have strayed in from 38:3 and 40:7.

At this point a probing question naturally arises: What can a work in such disorder do for us? A reasonable answer is, I suggest, that the very disorder can help it raise its fundamental question: *What is Justice and why should a man think he is entitled to it?*

In this disorder it reflects the very conflicts—the clashes of jarring hopes, fears, claims, and recognitions—that make man's questioning need for justice so great. In violent contrast to Job's own inherent rectitude—which Chapter 31 presents so nobly—the poem as a whole paints a grim picture indeed of earthly wrong and human ill-doings—as grim even as the account by Glaucon and Adeimantus in the opening Book II of the *Republic*.

Plato, though, comes through with his solution: an Idea of the Good coupled with a participation in immortality, and with allocations of reward and punishment, which long-continuing institutions have been able to conceive of and to accept. Does the Book of Job do anything like that? The answer should, I suggest, be "Probably not." Each reader, I think, the more deeply and discerningly he reads, will feel that whatever answer he finds has been of his own bringing. I, too, can offer here only what I have brought.

At the close of the poem, Shaddai has been roaring out of the whirlwind, saying, if magnificently, things that have been said already by Job or by his friends or by Elihu, but shouting them in a *taunting, scathing, sarcastic tone* which shows a dismaying inability in this utterer to conceive of or care about the situation of the human being he is addressing. The tone fully confirms what Job has foretold:

> If God is pleased to argue with him
> Man cannot answer one question in a thousand.

The typical question is:

67

Beyond

Tell me, you man of insight
Where were you when the earth was founded?

Shaddai ends with:

Can you thunder with a voice like mine?
Put on now your greatness,
Clothe yourself in *your* glory and power,
Let loose the floods of *your* anger,
Look on all who are proud and bring them low,
Destroy all those who are uplifted,
Pull down the wicked,

(All things that Job, through much of the poem, has been
complaining that the Lord conspicuously does not do.)

Hide them in the dust together,
Cover them in an unknown grave,
Then I will praise you
Saying that your own right hand can save you.

It is through comparing this utterance with what Job throughout the poem has been showing us, that we have to imagine
what Job—scrupulous, indignant, trustful, betrayed victim left
in an elimination camp—means by his final words.

While pondering this most famous crux, let us once more
attempt an overview of the difficulties. We have probably stressed
enough how frequently and with what resolution readers of Job—
both lay and professional—have ignored the tale-poem discrepancies, crushing the whole book into a preconceived, unitary
mold that does extreme violence to both. But now another and
far harder problem in whole and part relationships is on our
hands. *Ideally* (the italics are here to stress the differences
between what should be and what must be and is), a reading
of Job's closing speeches should fit not only what Shaddai has
just been saying to him, but the whole course of exchanges with
the three friends. Unfortunately, disorder in the text—increasing
as it advances—and uncertainties as to how this can be remedied
make any position problematic. Moreover, there are insertions

from other hands—the largest of them Elihu's contribution (32–39)—as well as a number of separate poems which, though they may be by the author, have not in general been thought to belong, among them Chapter 28. When these have been removed and the textual disarray dealt with as seems best, we still have an extremely indeterminate poetic body with which and against which to relate and adjust interpretations of the closing speeches. I put *interpretations* thus in the plural to remind us that the task is to distinguish between, compare, and balance what the speeches *may* mean, rather than to divine and declare *the* true and only reading. These are *closing* speeches, moreover; in addition to terminating the poem, they aim at *closure* in the *Gestalt* sense. What we should be doing is appraising, as fairly as we can, for these possible readings (pl.), their kinds and degrees of dramatic *and other* closures. And, unhappily for this endeavor, theological, devotional, and philosophic purposes can conflict, here more than with perhaps any other climax in literature. Edification, intelligential rectitude, the cleansing of the heart, other modes of catharsis, semantic decorum, respect for insight and for justice, the cultivation of sophrosyne—all these, which, *ideally* again, should seek a common good and offer mutual support, can be and have been sadly at odds. This, which makes the Book of Job so rewarding a field for study of mis-interpretations, and of the less creditable side of the politics of understanding and persuasion, also makes certainty as to its outcomes unusually unattainable. Whether this indeterminateness reduces or enhances the book's value is really what we have to consider. We may find that we conclude that Job's choice of silence after having seen the unutterable and Shaddai's inability to be relevant do jointly meet the poetic, moral, theological problem that generates the poem better than any ʾsolutionʾ that may be proffered as supposedly more edifying. And we may feel this even as clearly as we conclude that the epilogue totally fails to meet the problem set by the prologue. In both cases, what we select and appraise as an ending turns on just how we conceive the generating problem.

Beyond

The temptation waylaying every critic to invent a work for his author to essay, and then to either applaud his achievement or point out how he fails, is, or should be, well known to us all. With a work so far beyond our conceptions as Job, the temptation is especially strong. As a prophylactic, may I present the following exhibit, by a writer whose name has somehow slipped from me, which discusses one of the very few works that measure up to Job:

I should like though to call attention to Shakespeare's signal failure to make King Lear daemonic.

Lear has endured, etc., etc. . . . Should he not, having undergone all that, have become all powerful after having been all weak? This is what we want and expect after the storm scene.

But instead of becoming daemonic, Lear goes mad . . . This king Shakespeare tried to make divine but could not.

There are two remarks in *Lear* which relate to destiny, and they contradict one another.

> As flies to wanton boys are we to the gods,
> They kill us for their sport.

and

> The gods are just and of our pleasant vices
> Make instruments to plague us.

Clearly these remarks refute each other. The difficulty of thinking that both are true is the chief problem of Shakespeare's play and prevents it from being a true tragedy . . . The deaths in *King Lear* follow from conflicting principles. The work is simply not unified.

After a few deep breaths, let us return to consider what conclusion might be wide and high enough to unify the poem of Job. Can we find one in Chapter 28? This is a wisdom poem, which, though clearly misplaced, is thought by many Hebraists to be probably by the original poet and among his special triumphs. To Robert Pfeiffer, who offers a conjectural reconstruction of Chapter 28 in *Introduction to the Old Testament*, it "has no logical place in the Book of Job, unless it be the conclusion of

Job: Poem and Epilogue

Job's confession in 42:1-6." [7] He regards 28:28 as a gloss: "The philosophical implications of this chapter were obnoxious to Judaism." So placed, could it not serve as a turning point for something that might be called a reconcilement—not, however, between Job and Shaddai, but between opposed components in the structure of the poem?

In Job's first reply to Shaddai, "I lay my hand upon my mouth" may be read either as a fit gesture of humble and full submission or as an ironical and still quite unsubdued repudiation of what Shaddai has said as in any way a solution. The two parties who can enjoy such different views of the upshot or outcome of the verse drama must, it may seem, be quite different—as different as the Job of the prologue (1:21, 2:10) and the Job of the poem, who has so notably and repeatedly foreseen (and said so; for example, 9:14-17 and 9:3) that he would not, at the hoped-for critical point, be allowed to say anything. The two parties will be in the same opposed and antagonistic positions over almost every phrase in Job's final speeches. "Things too wonderful for me which I knew not": to one, this will be a properly penitent acknowledgment of his own (and man's) inadequacy. The other, who will note that Job, after all, has uttered these "things" (42:3), and so has the poem of Job still more, will find in these words the same contrast between "with his lips" and "in his heart." Behind the seeming submission, this party will scent the still unquenchable rebel, and will be inclined to take the alleged final verse (42:6) as an addition, a gloss appended by some person of less than the finest sensibility, precisely intended to squelch any such suspicions. But even if we give the verse to the poem,

---

7. Following his hint, in my dramatic rearrangement "Job's Comforting" (in *Internal Colloquies*), I have given a version of the chapter to Satan as an epilogue, adjusting 28:28 to accord with Plato's definition of courage as "knowledge of what is truly to be feared."
Destruction and Death say:

> "We have heard a rumour thereof with our ears
> To know what is to be feared is Wisdom;
> To keep from ill-doing is understanding."

I cannot see 28 as spoken by Job.

there still remains a great question: What is Job repenting? His former attitudes and utterances? But just which of them? They have been grandly various. And further, what in Shaddai's crescendo of derision should make repentance an appropriate response? Job has shown himself to be unforgettably courageous. He has frightened and enraged the friends with his audacity (9:20–22, 13:13–15):

Though I be righteous, mine own mouth shall condemn me.
Though I be perfect, it shall prove me perverse.
I am perfect; I regard not myself; I despise my life.
It is all one; therefore I say,
He destroyeth the perfect and the wicked.

Hold your peace, let me alone, that I may speak.
And let come on me what will . . .
Though he slay me, yet will I wait for him.

Are we to suppose that what he has now seen and listened to has been just too overwhelmingly terrifying (13:20–21):

Only do not two things unto me,
Then will I not hide myself from thy face;
Withdraw thine hand far from me;
And let not thy terror make me afraid.

That would be a miserable ending. A Psalmist may say (Ps. 51:17):

The sacrifices of God are a broken spirit
A broken and a contrite heart, O God, thou wilt not despise.

But it is not of Job that Psalm 51 is speaking. Not an excess of the terrific from the Voice, but too much that is incomprehensible (as deep insanity is) would better explain such a collapse. Less likely and even less appropriate, as a reading, is that of Marvin H. Pope, which concludes: "We must assume that Job is now convinced of what he had doubted, viz., God's providential care. . . . Now that God has spoken directly to him, Job's demands have been met" (*Job*, the Anchor Bible, p. 289). Have they, indeed? And why must we "assume" anything so totally out of character? What in Shaddai's speeches has touched in any but a contemptuous fashion on "providential care"? What in Job's experience had been anything but a denial of that? Job is as little a fool as anyone could be. What has Shaddai said that he could conceivably take as even hinting at "providential care"? The downpour of paralyzing questions from the Voice may more intelligibly be taken as designed to destroy any such hopes or expectations.

A larger and, it may be, more decisive consideration is invited. In the course of repeated study of chapters 3–31, 40:4–5, and 42:2–5, the attentive reader gets to know Job almost intimately— so far as close contact with one of the greatest of human minds is possible. In the course of chapters 38–41 (edit them as we may), what sort of mind do we feel is vociferating? Is it not well to reflect whether more than two thousand years' adoration of this utterance (however magnificent its phrases) might not have something to do with the sad state of the world and with the mad and abominable tyrannies which have so mercilessly infested it?

It will be plain that this debate between two minds—infidel and devout—over the conclusion of the poem and the evidence that could be adduced in support of opposing interpretations can be continued even to the length of Job's exchanges with the three friends. One is tempted to think that two such different views cannot meet, until one observes that they are, in fact, meeting again and again in Job himself throughout the poem. He is indeed in two minds, and from this the verse drama springs.

If the poem be so conceived, the sequel supplied in the folk tale becomes all the odder. But in any sane interpretation nothing in the poem that the Job of the poem could have said can be "the thing that is right" that "my servant Job hath spoken." Jahveh's values are too unlike Shaddai's to permit continuity. The more these differences are felt, the clearer it seems that the folk tale—if, indeed, it included Job's three friends at all—must have given to them and to Job speeches almost the reverse of those in the poem. The succinctness of the utterances in what we have of the tale is striking. The speeches in the missing middle section were probably as short as those in the poem are long. Essentially, Job must have rung further changes on 1:21 and 2:10, displaying the same exemplary patience. With patience in mind, more note should be taken of the patience the comforters have shown in 2:13. Seven days and nights amount to quite a time, for them, to remain speechless. But at last, we may imagine, even their forbearance breaks down and, in effect, they advise him as his wife, Dinah,[8] does in 2:9. Why not be done with his torments and put an end to it all? Or, at least, they might turn on him with something of the spirit of protest that in the Job of the poem so shocks and pains them. Something of this sort is needed to earn for them Jahveh's rebuke and his command that they make ritual request to Job to pray for them. It is part of Job's reward that his intercession for them is thus required and accepted. Deeper meanings than this have, however, been found. Exegetes, we know, can find *any*thing. "While the Job of the Dialogue apparently has no thought of suffering vicariously for the friends, or for anyone else, the Job of the Epilogue is placed in the line of development of the Christian doctrine of the Cross, though still a long way from it" (Marvin H. Pope, *Job*, the Anchor Bible). Happily, the length of the way is here remarked on!

The dreadfully shrewd art of this folk tale is seen again when Job's brethren and sisters and the rest (of whom we have hitherto heard nothing) appear with their money and their rings of gold

8. Commentators outdo one another, even the author of the tale, on poor Dinah. She "by a touch of quiet humour is spared" (when all her children, as ruthlessly as Niobe's, are destroyed); "she seems to be recognized by Satan as an unconscious ally." As to Job's feelings at his children's loss, he "emerges unscathed spiritually from the first trial" (Rabbi Dr. Victor E. Reichert, *The Soncino Bible*). It is interesting indeed to reflect on the variety of moral judgments great literature can elicit. How widely the meanings of the words men most confidently rely on—here, of *spiritually*—may wander! We have to thank Jung for insisting on Jahveh's need for *contrition*. We have also to note how singular Blake is in rejecting—as unspeakably impossible—any actual death of Job's children, and in making Dinah cosufferer with Job in his afflictions. How far beyond most of the commentators he is in his moral sense!

to bemoan and comfort him "concerning all the evil that the Lord had brought upon him." They come as soon as they realize that he is becoming again "the greatest of all the children of the east." Truly, "To him that hath shall be given." We see why Coleridge called the Bible *The Statesman's Manual.*

Having these great oppositions among attitudes in our minds, it is useful to compare with them another set of contrasts—those that served Plato as the mainspring, the tense bow, of the *Republic.*

4

Job and the *Republic*

The main theme of the *Republic* is initially proposed in the great speeches of Plato's brothers [1] at the opening of Book II, to which the rest is Socrates' reply. He has just somehow—"like a snake-charmer," says Glaucon—silenced Thrasymachus, who has been deriding Socrates for not knowing that justice is only what powerful enough people have found they can profit from. Glaucon is not satisfied. He sets out to state Thrasymachus's position properly—not as his own, but as the case that Socrates must really demolish. He must set aside all questions of rewards and punishments and show them what justice and injustice are in *themselves*. What *are* rightdoing and wrongdoing? What—apart from all other consequences—do they do to those who practice them? Socrates has been thinking all his life about these things. And now he must make the brothers and the company see why justice is good and injustice bad. It is in response to

1. Glaucon and Adeimantus are back from a battle of Megara, variously dated 424 B.C. and 409 B.C. Of the Poem of *Job*, the dating is somewhere between 700 B.C. and 200 B.C. Pfeiffer concludes that 608–580 B.C. may be most probable.

this plea that Socrates remarks that "there is nothing a man of sense would care more to talk about again and again." The outcome is the founding book of the Occidental mind.

In their two speeches the brothers outline, though in their highly different terms, the heart of the debate between the friends and Job as—in yet other terms—Socrates propounds, though he does not answer, the rending question of the origin of evil: the source of Job's inner struggle with himself. He has almost as little to say on *that* as even Shaddai. The two presentations, in spite of the immense difference in their presuppositions, are strangely complementary. If we can contrive to view them together— through a wide-enough-angle [2] lens—each set of oppositions (mutual dependencies) can become clearer.

Job's and the friends' views as to the fates of the righteous and the wicked in this world have not been—we will have noted— quite constant. Job certainly fluctuates as his own situation comes more or less burningly home to him. And the friends shift in their feeling that it may be a long while before the wicked get what they deserve. What is being considered, however, by both is what they take to be the facts, and they have to square them with (opponents of the friends would say "cook them to suit") their concepts of Shaddai.

When Glaucon sets up a traditional "immoralist" position for Socrates to overthrow, the situation is different. He is presenting not his own view, but one which might be widely held. It has indeed been often put forward, by Spinoza for example: "*Apart from society,* there is nothing which, by universal consent, is good or evil, since everyone *in a natural state* consults only his own profit." (My italics.) Glaucon is presenting this view, as Paul Shorey pertinently reminds us, for the first time. "There exists not a shred of evidence that any contemporary or predecessor of Plato could state any of their theories which he assailed,

2. This image appears, I take it, in Bacon's remark: "He that cannot expand and dilate the sight of his mind as well as narrow and contract it, wanteth a great faculty." This faculty, we may think, is chiefly in need of suitable exercises and may be cultivated and developed.

as well, as fully, as coherently, as systematically, as he had done it for them" (Introduction to the Loeb Classical Library translation of Plato's *Republic*, p. ix). In Book II of the *Republic* (358E):

> This is what men say justice is and what it comes from: *by nature* to do wrong is good, to suffer wrong is evil; but the evil of undergoing wrong is far greater than the good gained by doing it. So, having tasted both, those without the power to do wrong to others or to keep from being wronged by them agree to put an end to both. So law and order and, with them, society, start.

By nature? (My italics.) The wider and deeper the surveys of the anthropologists extend, the more doubtful the supposedly *natural* characteristics of human beings become. Comparisons between societies do not sustain such assumptions. Nor do appeals to what is being learned about the primates. Spinoza's first clause indeed gets increasing anthropological support. But his premise that everyone (in some supposed state) consults only his own profit is the choice of a recluse. Equally unreal in a different way is Glaucon's straw dummy. If we compare them with actual human beings described by an experienced observer, we see this. Let us try R. L. Stevenson:

> Poor soul, here for so little, cast among so many hardships, filled with desires so incommensurate and so inconsistent, savagely surrounded, savagely descended, irremediably condemned to prey upon his fellow lives: who should have blamed him had he been of a piece with his destiny and a being merely barbarous? And we look and behold him instead filled with imperfect virtues: . . . sitting down, amidst his momentary life, to debate of Right and Wrong and the attributes of the Deity . . . To touch the heart of his mystery, we find in him . . . the thought of Duty; the thought of something owing to himself, to his neighbour, to his God: an ideal of decency, to which he would rise if it were possible; a limit of shame, below which, if it be possible, he will not stoop . . . It matters not where we look, under what climate we observe him, in what stage of society, in what depth of ignorance, burthened with what erroneous morality; by camp-fires in Assiniboia, the snow powdering his shoulders, the wind plucking

his blanket, as he sits, passing the ceremonial calumet and uttering his grave opinions like a Roman senator; in ships at sea, a man inured to hardships and vile pleasures . . . in the slums of cities, moving among indifferent millions to mechanical employments . . . a fool, a thief, the comrade of thieves, even here keeping the point of honour and the touch of pity, often repaying the world's scorn with service, often standing firm upon a scruple, and at a certain cost rejecting riches:— everywhere some virtue cherished or affected, everywhere some decency of thought and carriage, everywhere the ensign of man's ineffectual goodness:—ah! if I could show you this! if I could show you these men and women, all the world over, in every stage of history, under every abuse of error, under every circumstance of failure, without hope, without help, without thanks, still obscurely fighting the lost fight of virtue, still clinging, in the brothel or on the scaffold, to some rag of honour, the poor jewel of their souls! They may seek to escape, and yet they cannot; it is not alone their privilege and glory, but their doom; they are condemned to some nobility; all their lives long, the desire of good is at their heels, the implacable hunter. . . . ("Pulvis et umbra") [3]

This is truly a grandly expanded, detailed, illustrated account of what Socrates, at the summit of his argument (Book VI, 508–09), is to startle Glaucon with:

Socrates: This, then, every soul looks for, and for this every soul does all that it does, feeling in some way what it is, but troubled and uncertain and unable to see clearly enough. The soul forms no fixed belief about the good as it does about the other things. For that very reason, it does not get any possible profit there may be in those other things.

Glaucon: Let me beg you, Socrates. Don't turn away now when you are so near. It will be enough for us if you do with the good what you have done with justice, temperance, and so on.

Socrates: It would be more than enough for me. No, my friend, let us put aside, for the present, the question of the true being of good; for to get to what is in my thoughts now about that seems to be an undertaking higher than the impulse which keeps me up today. But

3. "Duty," No. 169, from Bridges' anthology *The Spirit of Man.*

of what seems the offspring of the good, and most like it, I am willing to talk if so you desire. If not, we will let it drop.

Glaucon: Go on and make the full payment—the account of its father —another time.

Socrates: I would that I were able to make, and you to take, the full payment and not only the interest. But, at least, here is the interest, the offspring of the good. But be careful I don't mislead you with a false account of this interest.

Glaucon: We will take care of that. Go on . . .

Socrates: Which of the gods of the sky will you name the maker and cause of light which makes vision beautifully see and things be seen?

Glaucon: Why, the one you and all the others would name, for you are clearly talking about the sun . . .

Socrates: The sun, then, is what I named the offspring of the good which the good begot to be the parallel to itself. It was to be to seeing and the things which are seen what the good is to thought and to what thought is of. . . .

The sun, wouldn't you say, not only gives a thing its power to be seen, but its generation and growth, though the sun is not itself generation? So too, you are to say, things are known only because the good is present; that they are and what they are come from the good. But the good is not being, but is far higher in honour and power.

Glaucon: Heavens! That out-tops everything!

Socrates: You forced me to say what my thoughts were about it.

Glaucon: Don't stop. But do at least stretch out the parallel with the sun, if there is anything you are not giving us.

Socrates: Well, in fact, I am letting more than a little go.

Glaucon: Don't let the least bit.

Socrates: I fear I'll have to, but, as far as I may, I won't willingly overlook anything.

It will be apparent that we are in a calmer world of intellectual accomplishment from that other in which the poet of Job is the great master. Nonetheless, his quest and Plato's quest are radically the same. Something central to the human endeavor is trying to see. (Both poets are, at their climaxes, concerned about vision; both take the metaphor from optical to spiritual discernment as essential.) What must be seen is what *the quest itself* is and how it is *dependent on* and to what degree *free from*—something which Job, with a most ambiguous gesture (putting his hand over his lips), declines any longer to complain against or to dispute with, and which Socrates, in a different key, declares to be "higher than the impulse which keeps me up today." One thing common to these so different apices of insight is a concern with freedom. Neither the poet of Job nor Plato gives much *explicit* discussion anywhere to concepts, as such, of freedom; but they are both penetrated through and through by the sense of how central, to all they live for, self-control must be. Job follows up his opening curse with a prayer for death: "There [in Sheol] the prisoners are at ease together/They hear not the voice of the taskmaster" (3:18), and his apology (Chapter 31) is a poem illustrating noble qualities of control in counterpoint to the denounced ignoble freedoms of the Miscreants. So, too, Plato in the *Republic*, from a high point indeed in its argument, defines sophrosyne (temperance) in these terms:

Socrates: Temperance, I take it, is a sort of beautiful order, a control, as men say, over certain desires and pleasures. So a man is said to be 'master of himself,' a strange way of talking, because, if he is master of himself, he is equally the slave of himself, for it is one and the same person who is being talked of.

Glaucon: Undoubtedly.

Socrates: Well, the sense of this seems to me to be that in the man himself, that is, in his soul, there are two parts or forces, a good one and a bad one. And when the good one has the upper hand and authority then the man is said to be 'master of himself.' These are certainly words of approval. When it's the other way, and the smaller, best part is overruled by the mass of the worse, then he is 'the slave of himself'—certainly not words of approval. . . . So temperance in a society or in a man is a sort of agreement or harmony as to what is to be the government.

"Everyone . . . consults only his own profit." "This, then, every soul looks for, and for this every soul does all that it does, feeling in some way what it is, but troubled and uncertain and unable to see clearly enough. . . . For that very reason, it does not get any possible profit there may be in those other things."

Beyond

Socrates is giving a new depth to what *profit* may mean, looking beyond "those other things" in a truly awe-awakening fashion—though characteristically he is at the same time declining, as much as Job did, to say anything further. He will talk instead about, and explicitly with, an image: the offspring of the Good, the sun. And he is able to say through this most ancient, primeval, and traditional of all images more than Glaucon is begging him to say directly.

Job in his great apology (31:26–28) has been careful to defend himself against any charge of idolatry; his heart has not been secretly enticed. (Then, too, he has laid his hand upon his mouth.) But there are many degrees of idolatry and we are not so readily clear of it as we may suppose. Socrates, too, has been careful. Perhaps some sentences from Gilbert Murray, where he is talking of the Stoics, offspring of Socrates, and their possible attitudes towards the Olympian religion, may serve us here. (I have used them before but I know of no more relevant remarks on this great theme: the reaching never reaches.) Probably Murray had the above passage from the *Republic* on the Idea of the Good, along with so much else, in mind as he wrote:

They are not gods in whom anyone believes as a hard fact. Does this condemn them? Or is it just the other way? . . . You know that all your creeds and definitions are merely metaphors, . . . Your concepts are, by the nature of things, inadequate; the truth is not in you but beyond you, a thing not conquered but still to be pursued. Something like this, I take it, was the character of the Olympian Religion in the higher minds of later Greece. Its gods could awaken man's worship and strengthen his higher aspirations; but at heart they knew themselves to be only metaphors. As the most beautiful image carved by man was not the god, but only a symbol, to help towards conceiving the god; so the god himself, when conceived, was not the reality but only a symbol to help towards conceiving the reality.[4]

Beyond even the concepts of the Good—the Universal which orders all universals, beyond any other machinery it may contrive as a help to itself in its conceivings, its bodying forth of itself,

4. *Five Stages of Greek Religion* (New York: Doubleday, 1955), pp. 77–78.

Job and the *Republic*

and its world—the mind, as has been said in so many cultures in so many ways, finds *Itself*.

Perhaps an instance of this finding, from yet another, very different culture, may serve as a further help. Attar, the twelfth-century Persian saint, in his *The Bird Parliament* has been recounting how his company of Birds are led back to "the Everlasting *One*" by Tajidar the Wise (the Phoenix). After terrible hardships, the surviving thirty, though they have been "blinded by the Curse/Of Self-exile, that still grows worse and worse,/" at long last arrive. In Fitzgerald's translation:

> Once more they ventured from the Dust to raise
> Their eyes—up to the Throne—into the Blaze;
> And in the Centre of the Glory there
> Beheld the Figure of THEMSELVES, as 'twere
> Transfigured—looking to Themselves, beheld
> The Figure on the Throne en-miracled,
> Until their Eyes themselves and *That* between
> Did hesitate which SEER was and SEEN.[5]

Different in so many ways, these vehicles, as different as the images we may carve; and yet so Job, when he appeals to a witness, a vindicator, a goel, a representative who is to speak for him and do him justice, sees him as on high (16:18–19):

O earth, cover not thou my blood, and let my cry have no place.
Also now, behold, my witness is in heaven, and my record is on high.

And he has been thought to look for this redeemer, this restorer, this Voice to vouch for what matters most to him—his *integrity*—within the very power which seems to be breaking him.

Is it too big a stretch to find—in another mood and setting, as other as they well can be—the same discovery in Socrates' jocular recognition (so remote from Job's agony), his playful revelation to Glaucon that the justice they have been to such trouble in seeking has been staring them in the face from the start? (431–32):

5. A. J. Arberry, ed., *Persian Poems, An Anthology of Verse Translations* (New York: Dutton, 1954), p. 169.

83

Beyond

Socrates: Glaucon, we are in a very foolish position.

Glaucon: How so?

Socrates: Why, my dear man, it seems that what we have been looking for so long has all this time been rolling under our feet. And we never saw it. We have been like men looking for something they have in their hands.

It has been so literally from the start. As far back as the very first sketch of the beginnings of a society we have (369):

Socrates: Come then, let us invent a state, but its maker in fact will be our needs.

Adeimantus: Clearly.

And when the society has been sketched (371):

Socrates: Now where, in this society, will we see justice and injustice? In which of these parts which we have put in?

Adeimantus: I don't see them, Socrates, if they are not in some need which those very parts have for one another.

Socrates: That may be a good suggestion, Adeimantus. We will go into it further.

When they do so, justice in the individual mind (in analogy with justice in a society) is the *integrity* that results when all its components—its desires, its sentiments, and its reason—are doing their rightful work, minding their own business, not interfering with but supporting one another. Not any conformity to a ruling imposed from without, an obedience to a laid-down law, but a *consentaneity* among its contributing energies as to how they are to order their collaboration—that is justice. To the analogy, so well brought out by Plato, between justice in a state and in a single mind, we can add two others: the wholeness, the integrity in the co-operations of the physiological participants, in terms of which medicine defines the *health* of the body; and the integrity which linguistic analysis can now discover—from the phonologic up to the semantic interinanimations—in a good poem. It is such an integrity which Job claims in Chapter 31 and for which the vindicator (19:25–27) he trusts in can vouch. And it is this claim that moves his friends to protest. They attribute his afflictions to it. We may recall Pascal's rather too neatly mathematical classification: "There are only two kinds of men: the righteous who believe themselves sinners; the rest, sinners, who believe themselves righteous." He, with the friends, is forgetting all those who are, and truly believe themselves to be, *both:* a sort which Plato certainly, and probably Job, too, would think included all mankind. Plato might add that this is one of the true beliefs which are necessary for attaining whatever degree of justice is possible to man.

In Book XXIV of the *Iliad,* Achilles tells Priam that two urns stand on Zeus's floor and that from one he gives to man evils, from the other goods. To this Plato makes Socrates very explicitly object (380). He concludes: "This, then, is one of the laws of the state which poets will have to keep, that God is not the cause of all things but only of the good." As to what *is* the cause of evil Plato is not explicit; what he says of it in the *Timaeus* and elsewhere does not lessen the mystery. Nor does what one of the most memorable of his students learned from him. Philosophy, visiting Boethius in his prison, is comforting him— not in the style of Job's friends. " 'No man can doubt,' quoth she, 'but that God is almighty.' 'No man,' quoth I, 'that is well in his wits.' " (Compare Job's last speech, 42:2.) " 'But,' quoth she, 'there is nothing that He who is almighty cannot do.' 'Nothing,' quoth I. 'Wherefore,' quoth she, 'evil is nothing, since He cannot do it who can do anything.' " This disturbs Boethius, who has had cause to know evil. " 'Dost thou mock me,' quoth I, 'making with thy reasons an inextricable labyrinth, because thou dost now go in where thou meanest to go out again and after go out where thou camest in, or dost thou frame a wonderful circle of the simplicity of God?' " She assures him that she neither plays nor mocks, and tells him he has no cause to marvel "since thou hast learnt in Plato's school that our speeches must be like and as it were akin to the things we speak of." [6]

6. *The Consolation of Philosophy* in the translation of I.T., 1609, revised by H. F. Stewart (New York: Putnam, 1918), p. 291.

Beyond

Whether this truly illustrates a lesson taught in Plato's school we may doubt. It can, rather, represent one of the dangers of the concept of omnipotence. In any case, it is clear that the contrast as to the source of evil between Plato and either of the authors of Job could hardly be greater.

5

Immortality and Justice

The contrast between Plato and either of the authors of Job as to their presuppositions about immortality is well matched by their assumptions about the source of evil. Any comparing of the Book of Job and Plato asks us to remember the depth of the oppositions of their most relevant presuppositions.

For Job, Sheol is the end. It has a finality which heightened rather than diminished his longing for it, following that tremendous opening curse upon the day he was born. Against the briefness of his days, swifter than a weaver's shuttle and spent without hope, the pressure of his certainty that he will cease to be and that not even his present persecutor, Shaddai, will then see him (Job 7:9, 21) almost breaks itself down. Selected verses from later chapters have, of course, been taken as evidence that for Job, Sheol will somehow not be the end, and their prominence in the Order for the Burial of the Dead has given them a sanctity and a liturgical power that can make detached reading exceedingly hard (19:25–27):

I know that my Redeemer liveth, and that he shall stand at the latter day upon the earth: and though after my skin worms destroy this

87

body, yet in my flesh shall I see God. Whom I shall see for myself, and mine eyes shall behold, and not another.

But, as a student soon discovers, these verses and 16:18–19—variously emended, restored, reconstructed, interpreted, and rendered by equally competent, skilled, resourceful, and ingenious authorities—have been made to say too many things.

As on a map in the underground or subway or métro where too many searching fingers have rubbed off the surface just on the spot one would most wish to see it, so here—as at too many places in ancient texts—there is chaos in place of clarity. The deficiency increases with the possible importance of the message.

These passages have been traditionally received but often as being the only places in the Old Testament where any hope or promise of a life after death is offered. Accordingly, they take on an immensely significant role as focal points at which we can best watch the interplay of the forces producing such beliefs. As usual, these beliefs can differ widely. Behind the same formulations can be found the lowest and meanest as well as the loftiest and most noble of impulsions. A wish to be paid for being virtuous, for the sacrifices would-be right living exacts; a craving for vengeance to be visited upon one's enemies—these contrast sadly with the dismay, the pity and terror through which suffering can awaken in the observer the strongest impersonal demands for redress. For example, this passage of Coleridge's in *The Friend* (vol. 1, p. 147) on Tom Wedgwood:

Were it but for the remembrance of him alone and of his lot here below, the disbelief of a future state would sadden the world around me and blight the very grass in the field.

And sometimes, alas, far from creditable motives mingle with and disguise themselves as the altruistic; the theme is grievously familiar.

A less familiar study considers how far the nobler, indeed the noblest, forms of man's love of justice are affected by doctrines and beliefs—even when no more than half held—as to rewards and punishments in an afterworld. How, too, are the hopes and fears themselves, the rages and sorrows these doctrines address, derive from, and would satisfy, how are these modified by belief in an afterlife, a Heaven-Hell 'justification' of this world's wrongs?

In the *Republic,* and again as a startler for Glaucon, an affirmation is put into Socrates' mouth that could hardly be more assured (608C, D):

Socrates: But we have still said nothing about the greatest rewards of virtue.

Glaucon: Can there be other things greater than these we have talked of?

Socrates: What great thing may a little time take in? One lifetime is small in comparison with all time.

Glaucon: It is nothing.

Socrates: What then? Should an eternal thing be seriously troubled about anything so short, rather than about all time?

Glaucon: You are right. But why do you say this?

Socrates: Have you not seen that our souls live for ever and never come to an end?

Glaucon: No, by Zeus, I haven't. Are *you* able to say that?

Socrates: How would I not? And you may, for there is nothing hard about it.

The tone of certainty here seems stronger than with the parallel passages in the *Phaedo,* perhaps because Plato is there reporting Socrates' actual behavior and Socrates is being especially careful not to let his approaching death overmuch sway his judgment. He is going so soon to know, perhaps, or not know; and he has Cebes and Simmias before him and Phaedo beside him—a more sophisticated and more exacting audience than even those present in the *Republic.* In the scene, too, may be noted what seems in Socrates a personal relation with Apollo, not shown in the same way elsewhere.

The passage in the *Republic* follows the dismissal of Homer and leads on to the myth of Er. Though not quite as dim as Sheol, neutral and near-a-nothingness, Homer's afterlife for the shades has as little relevance to the injustices that afflict the living. On these, Glaucon, has begun in his first speech (II, 360–362) with thoroughly grim pictures of the thriving ill-doer and the persecution of the worthy; they are realistic enough to match any that Job and his friends [1] set forth and they are elaborate enough to make Socrates interject: "My word, Glaucon! You are polishing up your two men as if they were statues going in for a competition." It is truly striking how these accounts of what went on in Glaucon's time in Athens and in Job's time in Edom tally. Together they give us solid ground for asking: What sort of a world are we in? What sort of morality (if any) can lie behind its governance (if any)? Job, with no prospect of compensation in another life (or with at the most a faint and fleeting hope), answers: "Nonetheless good is good, evil evil: the rest is beyond me!" The *Republic* agrees with the first clause, adds its account of justice, and then proposes, in mythic mode, a solution: "The appalling unfairnesses of living may be explained by supposing that we have a series of lives separated by periods of reward and punishment." Otherwise all would be as unintelligible as Job (in 42:3) may have found it.

Socrates makes it as clear as anyone ever could that any detail introduced in depicting this scheme of compensations is mythologic. What about the scheme itself? Is that metaphorical, too? Is it as much of an allegory as that embodied in *The Divine Comedy*—"only a symbol," as a statue may be only a help in conceiving a god; "not the reality but only a symbol to help toward conceiving . . . ?"

Two reflections here may serve as helps; one is simple, the other not. The simple reflection is that the problem of injustice is not solved by Plato's scheme; it is only made more complicated. Evil in a series of lives, however numerous, is as hard to explain as evil in one life. Perhaps this reflection accounts for the fact that the successive incarnations scheme—though Plato suggested it so memorably—has rarely been taken up since Christianity

---

1. It seems likely that the accusations that Eliphaz seems to hurl at Job (22:5–20) are mistakenly translated, and are really a description of Everyman. If so, they would the better parallel what Glaucon sets up.

opted for the far more dramatic scheme of one life with a variously depicted everlasting to follow.

The not so simple reflection perhaps helps to make both Job's visions of his vindicator and heavenly witness and some of Plato's mythmaking more comprehensible. It starts from a conjecture that flickers in Job—though indirectly and insecurely—that perhaps his very protests, his rages of indignation, his certainties of his own intellectual and moral rectitude, his judgments of Shaddai are put into him, along with all else, by Shaddai. They could thus seem to be no more Job's revolt against Shaddai than Shaddai's criticism of himself. If this were to be pressed, the gap and the opposition between Job and Shaddai would be bridged. It must be stressed, however, that Shaddai's own words (38; 40:1, 2, 6–14) are such as to make this supposition untenable unless it is another Shaddai who answered out of the whirlwind. I will borrow a persuasive statement of the general situation from a quite different universe of discourse.

The individual who knows is here wrongly isolated, and then, because of that, is confronted with a mere alien Universe. And the individual, as so isolated, I agree, could do nothing, for indeed he is nothing. My real personal self which orders my world is in truth inseparably one with the Universe. Behind me the absolute reality works through and in union with myself, and the world which confronts me is at bottom one thing in substance and in power with this reality. There *is* a world of appearance and there *is* a sensuous curtain, and to seek to deny the presence of this curtain or to identify it with reality is mistaken. But for the truth I come back always to that doctrine of Hegel, that "'there is nothing behind the curtain other than that which is in front of it." For what is in front of it is the Absolute that is at once one with the Knower and behind him.[2]

The collocation of two such different presentations can, I am hoping, heighten a reflective awareness of whatever they may jointly present. Job can bring a dramatic immediacy to the situation Bradley is describing. But Bradley can generalize the fleeting conjecture that Job seems at times about to entertain.

2. Bradley, *Essays on Truth*, p. 218.

Beyond

Before and while pursuing these comparings, we should remind ourselves that the situation with which Bradley and Job are, however differently, both concerned is also that in which I write and you read, and is in fact inescapable.

A further reflection may be in place. If we take this identity (as in Attar-Fitzgerald) of what may be *seeing* with what may be *being seen* to heart, we should recognize its less reassuring possibilities. Theologians have balanced the rival claims that man is an image of his God and that his God is an image of man. They have not been, with rare exceptions, as ready to ponder the corresponding propositions in which some sort of a Satan replaces God. But in some self-searchings it may be easier to suppose that what faces us so guardedly in the mirror is the Adversary rather than either Jahveh or Shaddai.

To return to Hegel. Here again, as with the Book of Job and the *Republic*, a rather wide-angle viewing is required to compare things talked about in such different sorts of language and within such different frames of reference. Shaddai, whether when speaking or when figuring, both in Job's conceiving and Job's imagery, as General of the hostile forces, is as far as possible from being "a mere alien Universe." The collocation is, in this respect, a way of stressing the extraordinary degree of personality with which Job invests his world. And yet, in contrast with the folk-tale Jahveh—relatively very much a blown-up man—what a universal and cosmic force this creative Shaddai is! And Job knows this. It is part of his complaint (9:32):

> He is not a man, as I am, that I should answer him,
> That we should come together in judgment.

And yet Job and Shaddai do so come together and the outcome is a singular and reverberant absence of any meeting of minds. Job has repeatedly asserted that Shaddai will not answer his charges. Again and again he has been rehearsing in imagination for the confrontation, staging it in opposing ways and giving it opposing outcomes, certain sometimes of triumphant acquittal and sometimes of condemnation—an indication, this, probably of

Job's agonizing realization that his deepest complaints will not be answered. Since Shaddai is not a man, an argument—as in a trial—between Job and Shaddai is not possible. Something in Job has known all along that it is vain to think that he should effectively arraign Shaddai or that Shaddai should answer him. And the Voice out of the whirlwind is a perfect confirmation. One of its later echoes may be in Spinoza's judgment that human morality is as like divine morality as a dog is like the dog star. The failure in mutual comprehension seems, moreover, to be Shaddai's fault rather than Job's.

Let me revert here to the episode with which my discussion of the *Iliad* began: Athene's intervention to prevent Achilles from killing Agamemnon. She is unseen by any but him. Similarly, there is no sign in the poem of Job that anyone but Job either heard or saw Shaddai. Furthermore, it will be recalled, Athene shows clearly enough that she does not at all understand Achilles. She imagines motives in him that are just not there. Agamemnon's glorious gifts to come—three times as great as his present loss—are simply not relevant (for Achilles) to the situation Agamemnon has put him in. But the goddess supposes they should count greatly with the man she thinks she is talking to.

So here. As Athene addresses a person who is much more like herself than like Achilles, so Shaddai howls down a Job who is not to be found anywhere in the poem; a Job, too, who seems to be more like Shaddai himself, a would-be rival, a competitor, than like the man who has been asking for justice. The Voice from the whirlwind speaks, indeed, in strangely manlike tones, vaunting its admittedly matchless deeds, not unlike an Achilles boasting over a Hector. What the Voice elaborates, moreover, is, much of it, a derisive insistence on powers and claims that Job himself has already been taking no little account of (9:3–10). Different though Athene and Shaddai are—as different as Achilles is from Job—both divinities seem, in brief, to be thinking largely of reflections of themselves, seeing chiefly themselves behind the curtain.

Beyond

Such a personification of the heartless, mocking Tornado or Earthquake may appear to be far away from: "My real personal self which orders my world is in truth inseparably one with the Universe." Bradley's "real personal self"—thus given such high duties—is as *impersonal* as Shaddai's sarcasm is strangely *personal*. The capital *U* of *Universe* in Bradley is the only trace of anything remaining to match the powers supervising the worlds of Job or Achilles. And yet there is in the poem of Job (though *not*, as I see it, in the *Iliad*) more than a little that can bridge across to Hegel.

Among the later Psalms one especially, Psalm 139, can be read as making clear reference to the Poem of Job, indeed as a meditation upon Job's varying utterances about Shaddai, and a commentary that fits some aspects of them better than anything that Bildad or Zophar find to say. Eliphaz comes nearer than they can to the Hegelian component among Job's positions. Psalm 139, however, carries the speculative venture far further. It probes searchingly into much that Job has said that might well lead his revolt in the end to a complementarity situation. We may also be struck by the contrast between the addressee in the Psalm and the utterance of the Voice. A somewhat minute examination, using the Prayer-book Version (PBV), comparing it at the major points of difference with the Authorized Version (AV) and the Revised Version (RV) and with others and especially considering, too, Robert Bridges' (RB) "attempt to bring our magnificent Prayer-book version (from Coverdale's Bible of 1535) nearer to the original, *where that seemed desirable*" [3] (my italics) will be a good way of bringing out the ambiguities which perhaps *must* beset such reflections:

PBV: 1a   O Lord, Thou has searched me out and known me:
　　　　Thou knowest my downsitting and mine up-rising,
　　　　Thou understandeth my thoughts long before
　　　　　　　　　　　　　(AV: *afar off*   RB: *afar*)

---

3. Bridges' clause may usefully remind us that exact fidelity to an original need not override all other considerations. For example, authorities seem to agree that Elihu's intervention is relatively poor writing. AV makes it seem in places almost as good as much of the rest of the poem.

Immortality and Justice

2a Thou art about my path and about my bed:
(AV: *Thou compassest my path and my lying down.* RV: *Thou searchest out* RB: *Thou discernest my path and my bed*)

b   And spiest out all my ways.

> (AV, RV, RB: *And art acquainted with*)

3   For lo, there is not a word in my tongue
> (RB: *For, lo! ere the word is on my tongue*)

   But Thou, O Lord, Knowest it altogether,

4a Thou hast fashioned me behind and before:
> (AV, RV: *beset me* RB: *Thou dost compass me*)

b   And laid thine hand upon me
> (RB: *And over me Thou hast laid thine hand*)

5a Such Knowledge is too wonderful and excellent for me:
> (AV, RV, RB: *wonderful for me*)

b   I cannot attain unto it.
> (AV, RV, RB: *It is high, I cannot attain unto it*)

Already the relevance of the passage for any reading of Job will, I think, be apparent. And further, the power of the attribution of omniscience (or perhaps a preternatural degree of knowledge) remarked on above in connection with the folk tale— a knowledge which the Job of the poem does *not* at all so firmly attribute to Shaddai. Verse 3 here transfers the reference of "Such knowledge" (compare Job 7:8) from ˢʷthat necessary for creationˢʷ (Job 38:2b) to the specific instance of the speaker's own present and future thoughts and words. It is no longer what was done before Job existed (Job 38:18–21), but what is being done before and while Job speaks that is "too wonderful." The force and presence implied by the second-person *Thou* is heightened. What the lines are speaking *of* becomes immediately and literally that *to* which they are spoken and that *for* which they speak. (The RB variant of 4b brings this out more clearly: the capital of respect in *Thou* might in PBV, AV, and RV be merely the initial letter of the line.) This identification (of = to = for) holds with more poetry and high utterance than we customarily recognize. Commonly it proceeds through indirect, metaphoric, oblique means: the speaker becomes a mouthpiece (of = to = for) what speaks, what is communing with itself. But here this is literally so. Such an analysis may help to bring out both the cognitive and the affective-volitional daring here shown. The Psalmist is being extraordinarily bold and is inviting us, as auditors of this colloquy, to ask whence such courage comes.

As the variations in the translations help us to mark, there are deep ambivalences and tensions present—not only in the conceptions but in the co-operant attitudes conveyed:

2b	PBV: *spiest*	AV, RV, RB: *art acquainted with*		
4b	PBV: *fashioned*	AV, RV: *beset*	RB: *doth compass*	

If we describe these ambivalences with such terms as *acknowledge* and *resent, love* and *fear, submit to* and *resist,* PBV with *spiest* seems markedly rebellious. AV and RV with *beset* seem to join that party, too. *Spy* and *beset* are strong words indeed to find here. Espionage is a pejorative notion. The mind's privacy is to be jealously guarded as well as despaired of. And of *beset, Webster's* has "perplex; harass" and *Oxford English Dictionary* "to occupy (a road . . . etc.)," "to assail," among other senses, none of them very favorable. Compare "besetting sin." What comes up to the surface in these words is present and active throughout. It is doubtless inherent to the situation. There is that in the speaker which the utterance is trying to take account of and resolve—a duality of attitude or of feeling, at least.

Conceptions of Knowledge start out—should we not assume—from our own attempts towards it. The Psalmist, in imagining God's perfect Knowledge—an endeavor too lofty not to be defeated—is extrapolating, as the mathematicians say. There is a proportion, a ratio: As our more ignorant and self-deceptious hours are to those in which Knowledge of ourselves is at its clearest and fairest, so—but illimitably more so—is this *our* highest Knowledge of ourselves to God's. The first limb of this ratio recognizes our aptness to err, the last conceives a knowledge for which all error or darkness is impossible. The mistakes of fact,

the deceits as to motive and intention, the misconceptions of
every possible kind that enter into and shape our own views
of our own thoughts, feelings, wishes, acts are in this knowledge
seen with perfect clarity. And not only seen but understood—
what they are *and why* they are, all is accounted for.

These faults, errors, lies, sins are of both omission and
commission: *downsittings* and *up-risings*, both *path* and *bed*,
lying down. The change of order here makes it all cyclic: taking
on and giving up, startings and endings, round after round.
No wonder, then, that the human would-be knower of himself
shies away from, faints at, the thought of such knowledge as
"too wonderful and excellent for me" and feels a self-preserving
need, which can become overpowering, to remove himself from
such a paralyzing presence.

> 6a   Whither shall I go then from thy Spirit:
>   Or whither shall I go then from thy presence?
>   (AV, RV: *Or whither shall I flee you*   RB: *or*
>   *whither shall I flee then from thy face?*)

Here *flee* confirms the feeling of *spiest* and *beset*.

> 7a   If I climb up into heaven, thou art there:
>   (AV, RV: *If I ascend up*   RB: *climb . . . Thou*)
> b   If I go down to hell, thou art there also.
>   (AV: *If I make my bed in hell, behold,*
>   *thou art there*   RV: *Sheol*   RB: *If I lay*
>   *me down in hell, Thou art there also*)

The contrast with Job 7:21:

> For now shall I lie down in the dust;
> And thou shalt seek me diligently,
> but I shall not be

is very strong.

> 8a   If I take the wings of the morning:
>   And remain in the uttermost parts of the sea
>   (AV, RV: *And dwell*   RB: *remain*)

Beyond

9a   Even there also shall thy hand lead me:
     And thy right hand shall hold me.

> (RB: *Even there also should thy hand
> lead me and thy right hand hold me*)

"Whither shall I go then?" The answer, *for the Psalmist*, is,
Nowhere. There is no escape. And if we accept RB's *should,*
even his flight would be by God's leading. For most human
beings, other answers, escapes, and ways of downsitting are
innumerable and range from doctrines to drugs. This inability
to escape is a large part of what the Psalm has to say. Again,
the tension or ambivalence invites or imposes a twofold effort:
(1) To wake to, admit, realize, conceive (so far as possible)
and thereby expand our own limited capacity to know ourselves.
(We remember what *Gnothi seauton!* did for Socrates.) (2) The
inverse attempt (perhaps not separable) to wake to, admit,
realize, conceive (so far as possible) and thereby reduce our
capacities for error. In this second aspect of the self-searching
effort—the attempt, within our limits, towards an imitation of
God's knowledge—we may meet what can be grave dangers:
addiction to despairs, to disabling skepticisms—the pathologies
of consciousness and of conscience.

One way of balancing the daunting and the comforting components is by asking how the image "take the wings of the
morning" makes its miraculous contribution. Anyone watching
the dawn can, if he chooses, have present to him an immensely
powerful image of flight, of flight as a bird; flight, too, as hoped-
for escape—the edge of light endlessly flying from the too bright
day into hiding night. (This is especially so in a region as far
south and as readily scorched as Edom. And we moderns can
imagine the sunrise belt sweeping round the earth at 1000 m.p.h.
on the equator.) The complementing phrase is "and dwell in
the uttermost parts of the sea." We should not here overlook
the connections of *utter* with *out;* or, for *dwell,* its OE origin
dwellan, to wander, to linger, to tarry, or its kinship with O Fris
dwalia, to be in error, and with OE *dwolung,* doubt; also with
dull, which offers us *doldrums* (perhaps *dull + tantrums;* see

Partridge's *Origins*), and further connections with words meaning foolish and mad. What a contrast this drop is, this giving up
even of the flight! There follow the two most "compassing"
phrases of the Psalm (v. 10, AV): "shall thy hand lead me, and
thy right hand shall hold me." Even in taking those wings and in
the drop from that flight, we are being led and we are being held.
Not far off may be a doubt whether there is left us any autonomous "I" that can take those wings or "remain" or "dwell" in
those depths. We would then be undergoing that dissolution
and/or reconstitution that results from a sufficient realization of
what "Thy will be done" can mean: a loss, abandonment, jetti-
soning of the balancing, individual, personal will without which
"Thy," too, loses ("so far as is possible," Plato would add) all
its meaning.

And with the darkness and light of the next verses (turnings)
there are the same ambivalences.

10a If I say, Peradventure the darkness shall cover me:
        (AV, RV: *Surely the darkness*   RV: *shall overwhelm*
                                    RB: *may whelm me*)
    b Then shall my night be turned to day
    (AV: *Even the night shall be light about me*   RV: *And the light
    about me shall be day*   RB: *let my day be turned into night*)

With PBV and AV the sense closes with the end of the verse.
But RV and RB seem dramatically to confound the escapist more
completely. They seem to hand to him the irony—"And the light
about me shall be day"; "Let my day be turned into night"—only
to let him find himself refuted—"the night shineth as the day"
(v. 12). What seem to man the greatest opposites "to thee are both
alike"—alike, we have to note, as hiding nothing from God.

The dramatic contrast with Job is again very strong.

10:20 Are not my days few? cease then
        And let me alone, that I may take comfort:
                        (Heb.: *brighten up, a little*)

    21 Before I go whence I shall not return
        Even to the land of darkness and the thick shadow of death.

Beyond

22 A land of thick darkness, as darkness itself;
      A land of the shadow of death, without any order
      And where the light is as darkness.

So, too, at the end of the Psalm, after much that parallels the opening passage—including a statement on the fundamental question in embryology:

15a Thine eyes did see my substance yet being imperfect:
  b   And in thy book were all my members written;

16a Which day by day were fashioned:
  b   When as yet there was none of them

there is the same convergence of the daunting and the comforting. What can look like reckless self-righteousness:

23a Try me, O God, and seek the ground of my heart:
  b   Prove me and examine my thoughts.
24a Look well if there be any way of wickedness in me:
       And lead me in the way everlasting

can also look like an ultimate humility. There is in the challenge a recognition that this trying (this sifting) requires a knowledge too wonderful for him. With and in this submission—following upon his claim (v. 22) to be on God's side and to count God's enemies his—the Psalmist is admitted to a participation, the conditions for which he has been describing and displaying. That high knowledge he can and does, in his measure, attain to. To acknowledge that it is too excellent for him is part of it. He can still be led to know that there is no way out, however much at times he may mistakenly attempt to find one.

Before my quotation from Bradley, I suggested that it might help to make both Job's vision of his vindication and Plato's mythmaking more comprehensible. Myth may have been Plato's way of counterbalancing his unparalleled intellectual resource ("affluence," as Shorey calls it) with an equal liberty for the rest of himself, his way of protecting whatever such a power of thought might threaten. Besides the great formal myths—that of

Immortality and Justice

Er which closes the *Republic,* the parallel myth in the *Phaedo,* those in the *Phaedrus*—Plato has many others, some of them seeming to be mere images. Among them, that of the Cave (the "Cinema Hall," as it has been called) in the *Republic* (VII, 514) and the Pilot (VI, 488) are the most famous. Midway between these and passages fully lighted by logic, utterly awake and self-critical, are what might be regarded as but "likely stories," or even as no more than momentary emotive figures. One of these last—not sure itself perhaps whether to take itself seriously or not, whether to be theory or fantasy, or concession to traditional phrasing—concerns immortality. Partly for the reasons above hinted at, it has seldom, I think, had the attention Plato's other views have drawn or, were they not blocking the way, it might well claim.

Consider the passage (*Republic* VII, 534CD) following Plato's most explicit "account of the essence" of dialectic and dealing with nothing less central for him than the Idea of the Good itself:

Socrates: . . . if a man is without the power to do this, won't you say he hasn't a true knowledge of the good itself, or of any other good? Any shadow he grasps at is his through opinion, not through knowledge. Sleeping and half-sleeping through all his days, before he is awake he will come to the house of Hades and there sleep on forever.
Glaucon: Yes, by Zeus. I will say all that.

No doubt this may well be taken—as it has been by countless readers—as just a forceful way of saying: How much those who are not consummate dialecticians miss! Glaucon is unaware, as yet, of how Socrates is to startle him (*Republic* X, 608D) with:

Have you not seen that our souls live forever and never come to an end?

It should be noted, however, that this surmise, embodied here only in what may be considered "a mere metaphor," has its characteristically Platonic anticipations, as in his recommendation (VI, 498C) that the old when past the time for public work should

Beyond

freely range in the fields of thought and do nothing seriously but philosophy. So may they be truly happy when the end comes and crown their days here with a like fate hereafter.

Glaucon's comment is: "You seem deeply serious, Socrates." Plato's elder brother might well have been reflecting that Socrates, of all men, had found a way of combining the philosophic life with the most devoted sort of public service and that he, if any ever, stood the best chances of having his own days so crowned. What is distinctive about the passage from Book VII, however, is the suggestion that the alternative to the philosopher's immortality is an endless sleep. It is clear enough that proofs of the necessary immortality of the soul (could such proofs be contrived) are very different from a surmise that some may possibly come to win immortality by constant communing with "that which makes the divine itself be divine" (*Phaedrus*). The main contrast, though, is clear between this surmise (call it so) and the metempsychosis scheme—the recurrent reincarnations, punctuated by spells of reward and punishment, successive lives more or less [4] happy or unhappy as the preceding life was virtuous or not. In the surmise we have one life only; at its end those souls which have remained, or become, sufficiently like the divine source they come from, return to it. As for the others, they sleep on, dreamless (Hamlet should note) forever. On this final sleep Socrates' words towards the end of the *Apology* may only represent his personal feelings at that crowning moment:

With those who voted *for* me I would like to talk, while the authorities are busy and before I go to the place where I must die. Wait with me a little, my friends and judges—I don't mind calling *you* "judges." I'd like to show you the meaning of what has happened to me. . . . I have many reasons to think it is a good thing and that those of us who think death is an evil are wrong.

4. *more or less* because Plato's mythmaking faculty is careful to clutter the matter up with the highly numinous and dramatic business of the "sort of prophet" who tells the returning souls to pick their lots so that heaven may be guiltless and with the appointment, to each of us, of his daemon, or genius or guardian angel, lest we should somehow escape our fate.

Immortality and Justice

Among others, see this: death is either nothingness, complete unconsciousness; or it's a change, a migration of the soul to some other place. If it is unconsciousness, like a sleep in which you don't even dream, death is a very great gain. For if you take a night which you slept through without a dream and ask how many other days and nights of your life were better than that, I believe even the Great King of Persia himself would find that they were few. If that is what death is like, I say it is a gain. All time becomes no more than one night.

But if death is a change to some other living place where all the dead are, what could possibly be better? Think of meeting *real* judges there: Ninos and Rhadamanthus, and Aeacus and Triptolemus and the other demigods who lived just lives. Or, what wouldn't any of you give to meet Homer? I am willing to die again and again, if these things are true. And the greatest pleasure would be examining and questioning the people there, as I do here, to see which of them is wise, and who thinks he is when he isn't! What price would you pay, *judges*, to examine Agamemnon or Odysseus, or numberless others, men and women? To talk to them and be with them and go into things with them would be limitless happiness. They don't, at least, put you to death for doing it there. But, if what we are told is true, we go on living forever and are happier in other ways than we are here.[5]

He is exhilarated, in a mounting spirit, as one who has overcome a considerable adversary—perhaps his fear of the fear of death. And we may believe that Plato, who reported, or invented for him, these astonishingly characteristic expressions, would not be far from sharing his views. If death is nothingness, that Socrates, the most tireless man ever heard of, can call it a "gain" is significant. That is a judgment with which Job's shiftings of feeling about Sheol or, for that matter, Hector's or Achilles' feelings about Hades may usefully be compared.

As to the alternative to final sleep, Socrates is diverting himself and his *judges* with it. Doubtless most of them had gloomy enough faces. For all his playfulness—indeed exuberance—of fancy here, he knows very well when he turns his eyes another

5. Richards, *Why So, Socrates?*, pp. 29–30.

103

way and looks to the soul's "love of wisdom" (*Republic* 611)
that there is no imagining, much less any saying, what the future
life would be like to a soul that has thus escaped Sheol and won
through to immortality. As with a Redskin and his Happy Hunting
Grounds (Agamemnon and Odysseus are for Socrates his *game*)
or as though Hector and Achilles would still be warring across
some Elysian Fields, what we conceive of the heavenly must
always remain too human not to smile at us as we may at a
child with its toy. It is true even of Il Paradiso. The soul, if and
when it has "become as nearly like God as it is possible for a
man to be" (*Republic* 613) and thereby has *realized* as fully
what is implied by "being of the same family with the godlike,
the everliving and the eternal" (611), takes on inevitably a mode
of being beyond any knowledge we can reach.

This "candidacy for immortality" proposal might be expected
to have attracted more minds than in actuality it has yet shown
that it can. Perhaps its very reasonableness and its avoidance of
the monstrous have been against it. And yet—does it avoid the
monstrous? Does it not offer man a fatal ambition, the ambition
that the Tree of Life in *Genesis* (2:9, 3:22) has symbolized? One
of the deepest of all the Hellenic-Judaic oppositions appears
here: "By that sin fell the angels." We can let an equally divine
voice reply to Shakespeare for us:

> A life which realized this idea would be something more than
> human; for it would not be the expression of man's nature, but of
> some divine element in that nature. . . . Instead of listening to those
> who advise us as men and mortals not to lift our thoughts above what
> is human and mortal, we ought rather, as far as possible, to put off
> our mortality, and make every effort to live in the exercise of the
> highest of our faculties; for though it be but a small part of us, yet
> in power and value it far surpasses all the rest.
>
> —Aristotle, *Nicomachean Ethics* X, 7, 8

Is such an endeavor no more than "Vaulting ambition that
o'erleaps itself/And falls on the other"? Yet another divine voice
can speak to that:

Immortality and Justice

La donna mia, che mi vedeva in cura
forte sospeso, disse: "Da quel punto
depende il cielo, e tutte la natura."

My Lady, who beheld me in toil of deep
suspense, said: "From that point
doth hang heaven and all nature."

—Il Paradiso XXVIII, 40–2 [6]

Beatrice, who is Theology and so much more, is herself quoting
Aristotle here. And he, in his turn, is following Plato's account,
dialectically audited, of "the first principle that transcends
assumption . . . and is the starting point of all": the Idea of
the Good "from which all depends," [7] "that which gives true
being to whatever deep knowledge is of and the power to get
this knowledge" (*Republic* VI, 510–511). This account closes
Book VI and is at once followed by the parable of the Cave—the
translation into the imaginable of what has just been ideally
sketched. And when the Cave image has been further expounded
comes what Socrates finds himself able to give: "not the truth
itself, as I see it," but something like it.

For when what it all depends on is something which the reasoner
does not know, and the end and everything in between are put
together out of things he can't account for, how can any amount of
saying, "It is so!" be turned into true knowledge or science? [533]

This climax of frank acknowledgment leads on to the hint of the
philosopher's possible immortality with which this section began.

6. In general, the translations of *The Divine Comedy* are those of P. H.
Wicksteed (Temple Classics). I. A. R.
7. For the needed diagram (of the Divided Line) see Richards: *Plato's
Republic,* p. 119, and *So Much Nearer* (New York: Harcourt, 1968).

6

The Divine Comedy

Requital

The Divine Comedy, of all the greatest poems of every kind, is the hardest to be fair to, and for many reasons. It presents in the most uncompromising fashion, and with the utmost insistence, an unparalleled demand. And it supports its demand with an unequaled display of penalties for those not of its persuasion and of rewards for those who are: a display, of the one, so horrific, of the other, so exalted, that any word like *fair* or *just* comes to seem inappropriate—all very well for other worlds than that we have in this poem entered, but out of court here. And yet those other worlds are what it is judging and its central theme is requital: the most questionable element in concepts of justice. As much even as the *Republic* or the poem of Job, to both of which it has its forever-explorable relationships, it is an answer (the most threatening and compelling there is) to one of the most important questions any mind must raise. It is an answer wonderfully unlike theirs, and is offered in the name of, and with credentials provided by, an authority the poem itself maintains to be *beyond* all question—to be indeed the very source of questioning.

There are other well-understood reasons making fair dealings with it hard. Some are historical: the deep, as well as wide, changes that Hellenocentric culture has been passing through since 1300 (and these will continue). Some are doctrinal: the poem's connection with the institution most centrally representing Christianity, and its relations to positions departing from and opposed in various ways to that. It is the only great poem still tied to an organized, active, and self-defensive system of religious teaching. These are certainly factors to make approachers wary.

It seems likely that the problems of the role of beliefs in this poem have less to do with its author's certainties than with the institutions to which the beliefs it professes belong. As private persuasions Dante's beliefs may be in the same case as those set forth in innumerable other poems, many of them irreconcilably opposed. It is the fact that they have been, and for many still are, inalienable parts of Christianity that poses the question.

Minds that accept, totally or in part, the concepts of the cosmos set forth in the *Comedy* and minds that reject them, totally or in part—how can they sufficiently read alike a poem so unified and so precise? How can they reasonably be said to agree about many passages in it? How (to look closer) can they even disagree on 'it'? The possibles that *it* points to are too unlike.

This holds—though in varying ways—whether or not we suppose the articles in the Creed to be stating historic, factual events or timeless conditions; whether we take them as figuring aspects of the cosmos not literally statable; whether we take them as no more than inducements to attitudes and sentiments regarding ourselves and the world we would live in. The incompatibilities, the incommensurabilities that acceptances and rejections give rise to are not to be smoothed away by such reinterpretations.

At a time when immense advances in awareness of the inner

structure of the *Comedy* have recently been and are currently being made, we need especially to remind ourselves that questions as to its relations to other visions of the cosmos are likely to be neglected. No doubt the text—its sources, its references, the philosophical, moral, and religious background, much else about it and its age—can now be better understood than at any time later than when it was written. But are the largest over-all questions being given the attention the poem can rightly claim? The two inquiries should support one another. Knowing better what the *Comedy* is in itself, and as an outcome of its own age and frame, should help in seeing how it stands to utterances of other minds in other ages. And vice versa. But, as it has happened, when Dante's sources in the Bible, in Aristotle, in the Fathers, and especially in Aquinas have been noted, the question of how different his use of Aristotle, for example, may have become from what Aristotle would have approved is not pursued. An ungrateful remark perhaps, but it is more a recognition of human limitation than any sort of complaint.

There is, however, a tendency to make Dante studies, now that they have become so extensive, self-containing; and a shrinking from awkward questions about a work which gives so much is very natural. As no other, it takes the whole depth and height of disapproval and approval as its theme: from uttermost ugliness to supreme beauty, and with an entirety that is unmatched. Presented with so complete a range of human capability, we cannot reasonably be surprised to find—even deep among its impulsions—motives to make us squirm. Being so uncompromising—so absolute—in its judgments, it can hardly avoid arousing, in those who have come to have other positions for living, judgments in their turn no less severe. To many readers, of course, and among its contemporary readers, it has escaped some of these by taking as self-evident and axiomatic so many of the principles of condemnation and approbation adopted by the Catholic Church and held also by most of the Reformed churches. The heart of the problem is: How can a poem so dependent on

such principles be justly read by those who think them among
the most pernicious aberrations men have suffered? How can we
expect a fair reading from William Empson, for example, who
tells us that men "always try to imitate their gods, so that to worship a wicked one is sure to make them behave badly. But no god
had ever known before how to be so eerily and profoundly
wicked"? [1] We may think he overrates the bad eminence of Milton's God; but whether, and how constantly and how far, men try
to imitate their gods are questions we certainly should most carefully consider—though strangely we don't. I find myself doubting
the proposition deeply. Some sorts of people sometimes do imitate their gods; that is as far as I can go. Most people, if asked
the question, would, I think, be a bit taken aback. "How could
I imitate God? He is not a man as I am" seems to me a likely
and Job-like outcome of their reflection. Plato—in the *Republic*
—it is true, condemns much in the behavior of the Olympians
as offering bad models for man's imitation. Elsewhere, however, he does present a more exalted divinity as a good model.
And, of course, pastoral Christianity laments human failure to
imitate Christ. But these remarks feel over-remote. The mutual
dependencies of worshiper and worshiped are closer than the
word *imitation*—in its lighter uses—will suggest. I do not doubt
at all that traits in the worshiper often become embodied in
the god he worships (and vice versa) or that in these ways
human behavior can be immensely exalted or horribly debased.
Imitation can be subtly selective. I do not differ from Mr. Empson in thinking that a bad religion can make people worse than
they would be without it. On the other hand, noble natures
can select from even pernicious doctrine what can uncontaminat-
ingly support fine conduct. He continues, forcibly, "Until there
were enough influential and well-intentioned sceptics about, the
Christians could not be prevented from behaving with monstrous
wickedness" and adds, "since they worship as the source of all
goodness a God who, as soon as you are told the basic story

1. *Milton's God* (New York: New Directions, 1961), p. 247.

about him, is evidently the Devil." How, with such views, can he give the *Comedy* a fair reading? What would a "Dante's God" from his stern uncompromising typewriter be like?

But there are yet further reasons which make the *Comedy* the most challenging of all poems. I can perhaps group them and discuss them conveniently under three labels—though just what each label tries to collect and identify must wait for the discussion to display. I will set them down here as (1) 'Belief?'; (2) Incommensurabilites of comprehendings; (3) Reflexivity, self-involvement, of concepts.

(1) 'Belief?'. I have here to suggest that in addition to differences in *what is believed,* we have also to take into account differences in the *believings in which they are entertained.*

(2) How should we compare comprehendings, and typically, of these believings? Should we not, if and when we can, recall that

(3) Any principles we discover will apply, too, to these very principles themselves. As with *same* in my Prologue, the problems we are inquiring into reappear in our answers.

My three labels manifestly are not unconnected. I have made them three, not one, to illustrate the cyclic operation of self-appraisement: the self that would appraise has itself to be appraised.

These are, I suppose, the most arresting (and I am hoping the most repaying) of semantic considerations. Dante's poem seems to me to bring them up with peculiar force—but it brings so many considerations up so. That is its importance. In venturing an opinion, what, in the venturer, is at risk? Some of the opinions that will be appearing after a few pages will, there is no doubt, strike many a *Dantisto* as detestable and crass. I remember that *qui s'excuse s'accuse,* and I would wish my reasons for putting forward these opinions (and in what will be thought a very queer fashion) not to be taken as excuses.

"Judge not that ye be not judged." Dante was taught to judge by the "Scripture over him" (Il Paradiso XIX, 81–2), and by

the warped morale and the ferocious penal law of his day. We
will feel that we must make the largest allowances and do our
utmost to escape the implications of Matthew 7:1–2. How we
can best avoid judging and being judged in our own turn is
most succinctly put, for me, in a book title I once noted: *The
Psychopathology of the Seven Deadly Sins.* I seem to recall
laughing at it, being simple enough then to think it self-contra-
dictory. To remember, as constantly as we can, that vice is,
etiologically, disease can certainly be a strong support to charity.
The history of this most beneficent reform of a traditional and
inducive morality, this most noble extension of medicine, deserves fuller inquiry and wider study.

Judge is a word that repays close watching. Knowing, feeling, willing—in their combinations and their conflicts—are often
unusually open to study when we judge. The decisions are often
momentous enough to justify unusually careful examination of
our procedures—whether in court or in a lecture room. The connections with law (in all its senses) [2] incite unusually systematic and critical comparisons of cases. We are so often called
upon to judge how we judge, and answers to Juvenal's dismaying question *Quis custodiet ipsos custodes?* are so unsatisfying,
that ʷjudgeʷ may well serve as yet another type specimen of
words whose meanings we seemingly must know before we can
ask about them. This situation (predicament, quandary) is
familiar—with what ʷsameʷ handles, with what ʷmeaningʷ, itself, with what ʷinquireʷ and ʷknowʷ must try to do for us.
But ʷjudgeʷ may seem to have even higher responsibilities, no

---

2. Their range and intricacy are of course extraordinary. Even a cursory
tour, with the aid of, say, Eric Partridge's *Origins* (New York: Macmillan,
1962) through the cognates and compounds and derivatives of *legal* and
legend will show how nearly illimitable their applications are and how resourceful the interactions between them can be. Of *legal:* "The entire group
rests upon L. *lex* 'law,' originally religious and then governmental. *Lex* is
o.o.o. (of obscure origin)—unless, as is probable, it derives from L. *legere,*
to collect: for the latter group, see LEGEND." Between them they span every
possible way of talking, supposing, conceiving—of *interpreting* in the full
range of uses of that provocatively necessary word.

doubt because of reverberations from the apocalyptic implications of the "Day of Judgment."

In these three ways—(1) the institutional status of the beliefs on and with which it builds; (2) the incommensurabilities of the views of necessarily varying readers; (3) the self-applicable, reflexive character of its key concepts—the *Comedy* is the most challenging of the greater works the Hellenocentric culture possesses and can use in appraising itself. How we should read it is thus a peculiarly self-searching problem. How should we "make up our minds" about it, seeing (1) that all beliefs are in some ways and some measures institutional—they come to us from some segment of society; (2) that, since no two minds see alike, the question is: How deep are the differences? and (3) that the critique of seeings consists of seeings? Towards an answer we may reflect that "making up one's mind" is a self-renewing and perpetual endeavor, and that we should never lightly assume that we get better at it. That is just what we have to judge—for each successive attempt. The mind we make up may sometimes be demonstrably better in some respects, worse in others. That ʳdemonstrablyʳ is another of these reflexive concepts. Particularly should we remember that in comparing successive pictures of the cosmos (say those attainable in 1300 and in 1973), future as well as past pictures are relevant. What men have thought they saw and what they may come to think they can see both belong in the account. Both sets of pictures are conjectural; both depend upon what men think they see now. There is plenty in the record to remind us that these pictures are uneven; parts of them have, for long periods, improved, sometimes suddenly; other parts have deteriorated, and as suddenly. Needless to say, perhaps, its measures of improvement and of deterioration are the most important part of any picture of the cosmos, including that being formed here and now.

The measures themselves are subject to change. They are governed—increasingly, it seems—by such sets of conjectural pictures of the past and future. Men have gained in recent centuries increasingly available means of devising and diffusing such picturings. At this moment, the picture of the immediate —30-odd years—future considered most probable by the best informed, using the most powerful and self-controlling means of appraisal, is of an imminent collapse of the human effort through failure to change its measures fast enough. However, a far wider and livelier awareness of this estimate and of its grounds (a realization which modern media of communication could distribute and drive home in a few months) might bring about the needed changes soon enough.

It is within this frame and in terms of such analogy to a Day of Judgment that we will try to consider how we may best read the *Comedy*. That a reflective reading can be directly relevant to our present situation is what should be shown. If the procedure used seems strange, the intricacy and reflexivity and urgency of the undertaking is my explanation. Such an elaborate and apparently circuitous treatment is a tribute to the unity, compactness, and involvedness of the poem, as I see it.

I present a set of three cantos in *terza rima,* which vigorously *oppose* the prime concepts and sentiments in the cosmic picture offered by the *Comedy,* and constitute a *case* against them. I then proceed to a prose gloss upon this presentation. That this case is presented first in verse amounts to an experiment intended to support the view that more intricate and more highly organized meanings can be conveyed more adequately in verse than in prose. The prose commentary or gloss which follows I see as essentially defensive. Its duty is to guard the verse from misapprehensions.

I can best introduce my grounds for adopting this uncommon procedure by reference to the memorable, though indeed subversive, passage with which Dante closes §XXV of *The Vita Nuova.*

He has been discussing the licenses allowed ancient poets and vernacular writers in rhyme to use personifications and other figures of poetry. But the ancients did not so without reason;

Beyond

nor may the modern. I use here the translation of Charles S. Singleton, from his revelatory *An Essay on The Vita Nuova.*[3]

And in order that no ignorant person may grow arrogant over this, I say that neither the ancient poets spoke thus without reason nor must those who write in rhyme speak so, having no reasoning in them of what they write; for it would be a great shame to one who wrote in rhyme of things under the garb of figure and rhetorical color and then, when asked, could not divest his words of such a garb so that they might have true meaning. And this first friend of mine [Cavalcanti] and I know well of some who write in rhyme thus foolishly.

The contrast between this requirement of the poet and Socrates' finding (in the *Apology*) that the poets he interviewed were quite unable to explain their meanings should make us wonder. On the whole, poets through the ages have regarded as somewhat misguided any attempts to make them say *without use of poetic means* what they think they have been doing through them. So much so that their refusals to be helpful to would-be comprehenders have often smacked not a little of professional mystery-mongering. Dante's position here makes him a notable exception, both in his theory of composition and (I assume) in his practice likewise. That a poet of his resources, possessed of an equipment and a control of it equal to those of any, wrote professedly to such strict standards is certainly an important point for discussions of that perennial problem, the congruences in power and scope of verse and prose.

There is, moreover, an even more important reason for giving Dante's ruling here our very closest attention. I quote from Singleton's commentary.

Just as poems ought to resemble the creation, as we have seen, so poets ought to be like God. The world created by God is transcended by the Truth which is in Himself.

The argument here is of extreme interest for what it conceives the nature of poetry to be; or better, perhaps for what it insists that the nature of poets be.

3. (Cambridge, Mass: Harvard Univ. Press, 1949), p. 49.

114

The Divine Comedy

This apposition of descriptive and prescriptive formulations is instructive indeed. The first supposes Dante to have been declaring *what poetry is;* the second takes him as inviting or directing the poet to be such and such.

Singleton continues:

Let us recall what Bonaventura said about the Book of the Created World:

. . . suplex est liber, unus scilicet scriptus intus, qui est Dei aeterna ars et sapientia, et alius scriptus foris, scilicet mundus sensibilis.

So it should be with poets. Their art and wisdom should transcend their little creations in figure and color. In their minds should be the reasons for their creations. They ought, in short, to work in the image of God.

No resemblance in this sense may obscure, to be sure, the infinite difference. For one thing, God is not accountable and poets are. God may not be asked to say what the Truth about His creation is. Poets may be asked for the truth about theirs. And if they are asked, then it should be a great shame to any one of them if he were unable to show that, over and above his creation in figure and color, he knew the truth of his work.[4]

I have quoted so much because I can find nothing else which better illuminates (more clearly assumes, more plainly instances, more solidly affirms) the extreme differences between (1) the certainties of the Middle Ages (from which we struggle to free ourselves) and our own (on which our hopes of such deliverance may depend); between (2) our conceptions of God and of his services to man and the Middle Ages' conceptions of man and of his service to God; between (3) what they supposed themselves to be capable of knowing (and, in effect, to know) and what we feel equally certain that we can and cannot know (and do and in fact do not know), and between (4) their conceptions and ours of the relationship of a vehicle to that which it would convey.

To return, however, to the rivalries of prose and verse. Every

4. Ibid.

Beyond

self-critical writer of any verse which is at all strict in its self-set conditions must be constantly fascinated by this study—its interest being among the inducements to employ himself thus. It occurred to me that I could combine indulgence of these curiosities with a parallel study in literary tact. To make a full-scale attack *in prose* on the central tenets on which the *Comedy* is built—its foundation piers, indeed—while picturing the expressions and imagining the comments of *Dantisti* I count as close friends was not an enterprise I looked forward to. Plato himself—never one to underrate his debts—seems to have felt something of this sort in his rejection of Homer. It may be noted that when he turns around to possible concession, he says that if any could plead Homer's case *in prose*, gladly will he listen. Could he have feared the persuasiveness of sufficiently well-handled verse? However, less by conscious design than through obscurer promptings, I found myself using *terza rima* in English (a not unexacting form) as a means, not of softening any blows, but of assuming an impersonality, a detachment, and an authority no prose of mine would ever pretend to. Three cantos—each of thirty-five tercets, as it turned out—thus composed themselves. This is the most accurate way of describing what occurred. To begin with, I supposed *one* such canto would be sufficient, would be all in fact that I could manage and enough to fit the case. But this first canto rounded itself off with what was, to me, such surprising assurance that I began to suspect that another might be on its way. Just what it would be *about* was not as evident, ahead of time, as with the first. But it early declared itself to be purgatorial, and with that a fear grew up that a third, of some paradisal nature would ask to be written. This last seemed then beyond conceiving. However, both second and third cantos took charge and built themselves at a rate that left me somewhat breathless. Each was constantly well ahead of anticipations, and neither gave me cause, at any point, to wonder much where it was going. Each —Canto II within three days, Canto III within two more—shut itself down without allowing me any doubt that it was at its end. Some weeks later came a fair-copy period of a few days, with some smoothing out of rhyme crumples and strengthening of phrases. And that was that.

I mention these particulars to bring out that there was a compulsive, almost invasive character about all three that was to me most welcome. They were, I felt, serving as a means of *finding out what I thought* about matters that had seemed much less than clear enough before the verses put them in order—rather like efficient secretaries straightening out and tidying up my desk. Meanwhile, however, they had been raising for me a quite other sort of problem. I had been rereading the *Comedy* with a view to getting to work on a chapter broadly planned some years ago for this book. Here, suddenly, in place of that chapter I had written something else, something that looked for a while as though it might get badly in the way of any proper chapter. Then it occurred to me (again in an invasive way) that the solution might be through notes and glosses. Here §XXV of *La Vita Nuova* played its part. I had for some time been wanting to do something—simply as an experiment in literary semantics—about the verse and gloss relations in *La Vita Nuova,* and I would, I think, have written on them years ago had Charles Singleton's extraordinary pioneer *Essay* come into my hands. Now that it had, it brought me both an incentive and an opportunity to experiment, and a means, I hope, of clarifying somewhat the three-labels tangle touched on above.

What I have done, accordingly, is append to each of my cantos a set of notes and glosses, which attempt to show in prose what my verses (as I see them) would have us take them to be trying to present. As with all cases in which (through other words or any other signs) we attempt to explicate a sign (give it an *interpretant*—to use C. S. Peirce's term), sign and interpretant interact. Neither is or does what it would be or do if it occurred alone. In some degree (small or great) sign and interpretant gain and/or lose through influence from one another. And, for them as being so changed, new interplay can develop. There may thus be a continuing vibrancy between them.

Beyond

The written down gloss is sometimes *more,* not less, coactive with the original sign than interpretants that merely arise in the mind imaginally or are but schematically, sketchily verbalized. Being written, it can be read in varying ways. Interpretants that are relatively tacit are in more danger of being lost or of being mistaken for one another. But our experience should make us doubtful of rules in such matters. We can, however, surmise that often the *life* we feel to animate a sign may be from such vibrant interplay between rival interpretants—perhaps incompatible or even in seemingly mortal opposition. With signs that are complex, unified, and yet ostensibly unequivocal, could not such clashings between their interpretants have something to do with their continuing vitality? Opinions held about the *Comedy* are certainly diverse enough—and mutual regard among *Dantisti* polite enough—to encourage such a conjecture. It would indeed be no more than an application in literary semantics of an extension of the Principle of Complementarity that has proved of such service in physics. As, in the investigation of the atom, mutually exclusive experimental positions can in their outcomes be combined to give understanding and power far beyond any they could yield in isolation, so here, too—in this incomparably more intricate matter—irreconcilable approaches (theological and medical) may yet be brought into co-operation. There are combative impulses which would prevent it. By curbing them may we not learn how to see man's nature and destiny with more entire, comprehensive, and faithful vision? The possibility encourages experiment.

Whose Endless Jar

Down in the world endlessly bitter,
    and along the mount . . .
and after . . .
    I have learnt that which, if I tell it,
    to many will have strong bitter flavour.

        —Il Paradiso XVII, 112–117

The Divine Comedy

Desire in the beginning was made
One with the first cast of thought.
Searching their hearts' wisdom,
The sages found Being
Threaded in not-Being.

—*Rig Veda* X, 129

I

Red in the morning
Shepherds' warning

Mercyless cruel madness, to our eyes,
    Savaged this Seer blest, threatening the honour
    His due who could so people even the skies.   3

Say, rather, his World, which fed in him that humour,
    His World, it was, was mad; as ours too is,
    Though ravaged by far other codes of rumour.   6

His rumours told of God; were Theology's;
    Ours fan out from young *a b c*'s of Science,
    Polluted still by taunting strains from his   9

Still strong enough to tincture with defiance
    Our straight rejection, to create in us
    What can protect our weakness from compliance.   12

As we may think of him, miraculous
    His grasp of all that he could take as known,
    His use of it to shape his giant purpose: 15

Vessel in which his venom's less his own
    Than theirs for whom he bodied forth his dream,
    Their marrow rancours aching through the bone.   18

His vision took Creation's as its theme,
    Found Hatred in the very strokes of Fate:
    The primal motive of the deadly scheme.   21

Beyond

(Nothing can serve more than disdain of Hate,
    Remedy outranging love of Love.
    O still small voice! Let us not hear too late!)   24

Great hater was this poet, trusting above
    A Source of Hate, his hatreds to confirm:
    The very warp of the dread web he wove.   27

Would the cleared eye discern now Hatred's term,
    End it for good, the extirpatable,
    Surgeon it out for ever, root and germ,   30

It to itself must be inexorable,
    No mercy have on its own hates and grow
    To its self-ordering Self amenable.   33

Fount of Despair: that men can wound men so
    To bend them to what wishes! So began
    Delight from agonies. O, might we throw   36

That out to wry Time's avid ash-can,
    As with the fires that used to scorch Smithfield,
    All manic torments men can ply on Man.   39

Past all, the ways men have Man's will annealed!
    For sanction: that Great Soul's glowing tomb.
    Yet he, So Worthy, showed how slight the yield.   42

Let us regard now duly, those to whom
    An Eternal Torturer seems—O sick the soul!—
    Fit image still of what they dare presume.   45

Forgive the City of Dis; Hell's great hole
    Fill in. And that stuck Goblin framed
    As mock-up of its Maker—to rue in dole   48

Not reign in bliss—that huge, foul Chewer, blamed,
    With Eve, for Evil (though she, with Adam, be out),
    Insult with such strained cunning aimed   51

At treachery, what should that stir but doubt
   That worse betrayal far must here redound
   A grief too full for effigy to flout.   54

The specialty of rule; Justice, its ground;
   Source both and goal: Responsibility.
   Let Lucifer (and Eve) exceed set bound,   57

It was because they were so formed. If He
   Created them, His then would be the guilt,
   If guilt there were. Nor would to call them free   60

Absolve Him, their Designer. Grant He built
   Them free to seek, not passively await
   Knowledge to come, withheld; must Creation wilt   63

Through fault, if fault, of timing, Love turn to Hate?
   On that wreck Heaven and Earth! Infinite Mind
   In wanton rage! What less commensurate?   66

"Good measures with itself and has no end":
   Is not a prey to time. No ray of Good
   Out of accord with Good can be, or find   69

Another ray frustrating it, nor should
   Even Dante's rayings twist us so astray
   As to imagine any true ray could.   72

Chiefly, the "Scripture over you" did betray.
   There in your Limbo you might well have heard
   From "The Master of those who know" of a wiser way.   75

"True search for God is God's": so Plato stirred
   All the Academy to accept as sooth
   That God Himself through men saw God assured.   78

And Aristotle's Plato taught: "In truth
   God, who is purely Good, can no evil send
   On any. From elsewhere all cause for ruth."   81

Beyond

And Plato's Socrates had said: "Crito, my friend,
    Take heed. Do not assent to this unless you must,
    For this The Key is. Who on this contend   84

Can hardly not despise, contemn, distrust
    Each other. *Never by wrong, or threat of wrong,*
    May one defend himself, however unjust   87

The wrong done to him." This Socrates said long,
    Four centuries, before one harrowed Hell,
    After short life lost harrying the strong;   90

But, in it, much that—saddest truth to tell—
    Has worked in men much harm: augmenting Hate,
    Bringing a sword, not Peace. O Infidel!   93

Love your enemies: what strange call elate!
    Forgive them, for they know not . . . But some do,
    Who therefore in the Seat of Judgment sate   96

Decreeing all, the whole Inferno through:
    Each touch that earns Farinata's great disdain.
    Or would you doubt that Hell's real Emperors knew?   99

What we are we see through what we choose to feign.
    Yet must we change, find ourselves otherwise;
    May, sifted so, some innocence regain   102

And, knowing we fail, see, in our last Surmise,
    Failure widespread, yet blameless. To keep sane
    Take we our comfort from the imperfect skies.   105

II

Red at night:
Shepherds' delight

Green is the colour of Hope: what's now left green?
    What ranges of green, ask rather, now remain?
    Those of the greenhorn? What hopes might his have been?   3

Watching the leaves fall, think they bud again,
    Afresh unfurl, that now in high farewell
    Blaze up defiant, reckless, as though pain,   6

Endings of tasks, despairs . . . failings beyond tell
    Were but a cause for gayer wilder splendour,
    Fit refutation of the tale of Hell.   9

Let young sprays in their turn the round endure,
    Their tender leafit hopes unfold again,
    Burn up at last to close the cycle's grandeur,   12

Which serves long wider hopes out of their ken
    Who kept one tree alive. There'll be more trees.
    This is the clime and season for old men.   15

So let rain soak, frost cut, the storm-blast seize.
    There's nothing lost as the leaves sail away
    Some circling and settling, seemingly, as they please.   18

Hell was no hope but a Hope's shadow, say,
    That must decline before the shadow fade;
    With it the threat to make poor men obey   21

Laws cutting down their lesser hopes. Afraid
    Enough, would they turn their eyes toward
    The Recompence that for all losses paid?   24

In fact, they seldom did. Men don't look forward
    That far without reminders. So, from the first,
    The deadly scheme of penalty-reward.   27

The watchful eye of prophet, then of priest
    Espionaged men's doings. But there came
    "The greatest of all the children of the East."   30

This Job, his Jahveh's boast, one "without blame,"
    Unique in this, submissive beyond praise,
    Suffered at Jahveh's hand wrong beyond shame,   33

Beyond

Atrocious, wanton, "without cause." Though Jahveh pays
　　His immobile Job twofold for what's been done,
　　The wrongs remain. So do the divine ways.　　　　36

Job's poet, though, spoke—to say for Job what none,
　　Not Jahveh certainly, knew was in his mind;
　　That preluding Satan might be such a one.　　　　39

Nothing to do with Dante's fouled-up Fiend;
　　Nor merely Jahveh's Secret Service Head;
　　Nor even the Adversary unconfined;　　　　42

More still belike: he who—as what's living to what's dead,
　　So he to Jahveh—calls the Omniscient's bluff.
　　"Does Job serve God for naught?" was what he said.　　　　45

Rewards and penalties: to Job more than enough
　　Of both were dealt; of goods to hold his troth;
　　Of unearned griefs to make him as steel-tough　　　　48

As his great poet shows him. Thus his oath
　　Of innocence, his uttermost defiance,
　　Nonplus Shaddai, who can but boast in wrath　　　　51

So little to the purpose that the silence
　　Job then elects is well charged with disdain,
　　And is no sort of neighbour to compliance.　　　　54

Job's Comforters had had as their refrain:
　　"What just man ever perished? You must have sinned.
　　Humble yourself. Repent. Confess again,　　　　57

And He your punishment will then rescind.
　　Unrighteousness He scourges. The righteous thrive."
　　Till Job retorts, "Your words are but as wind."　　　　60

Such precepts grew the doctrine of the Hive
　　That settled in Judea. Deuteronomy
　　Laid down, almost, that here, while we're alive,　　　　63

Prosperity means God's favour, even that He
    Must hate the afflicted. Afterlife was none;
    So here on earth:—reward and penalty.   66

Amos had seen more shrewdly what was done,
    Watched the Great grind the faces of the poor,
    Making fine profit from it; warned such oppression,   69

Such Outrage, would bring retribution sure
    Upon the nation: This was God's word.
    It was their victims His chastisements bore.   72

The Prophets' words were what, as God's, they heard,
    Daring, through them, even to rebuke the Great,
    Who were not often—sad to say—so cured,   75

But, since death comes to all, early or late,
    And how men fare in Sheol's for all the same,
    Their own pet appetites and whims to sate,   78

Since they still had the power, stayed their aim.
    Who disobeyed, what they so earned they got
    From smiling Great impervious to shame.   81

It was the Tyrant's ways that led (God wot?)
    Plato to bring in (from India?) Hell
    For Ardiaeos the Great—"The Key" forgot.   84

So came the reminders prompt to make men dwell
    In dread foreboding on what Tyrants do.
    Earthly and Heavenly Rulers one another spell,   87

As Moscow's Anti-Religion Showcase knew:
    There, from one block, Czar and Icon blend
    Knout-deep, an indistinguishable crew.   90

"The Fear of God": the Old Testament to the end
    Knows no phrase else. Religion? Best obey!
    No image make! Make offerings! Don't offend!   93

Beyond

What Image this to which to have to pray,
    To worship, emulate, be misshapen by!
    What wonder men grew twisted, ruthless! They   96

Who, from a fairer model, might learn why
    Eve's wish to be like God must work out thus,
    So could conduct their steps to mount more high.   99

This is our Mount of Purgatory. For us:—
    To cleanse our hopes, rid them of what's our own,
    Shed *lives-to-come* like leaves turned poisonous,   102

Forego ourselves, keep troth with how we have grown,
    Accept our lot, greenhorns deciduous,
    And, since all acts are seeds, see to it well what's sown.   105

III

    Whence this created world came
    And whether he made it, nor not:
    He alone who sees all in the furthest heaven
    Knows or does not know.

                      —*Rig Veda* X, 129

Which daughter of Memory should I now invoke?
    She who is friendliest to hazardous thoughts,
    Dwindling the preternatural; who spoke   3

With the first flyers, with all Argonauts,
    With those confining Logic, with Niels Bohr:
    Archangels governed by least likely OUGHTS,   6

And she who strengthens in her servitor
    The self-detached, the apprehensive heart,
    The uncommitted, asking most of her: 9

Their rede I'd hearken now and from that start.
    Not mine to judge but theirs who this indite;
    Their soil, this page, for what they will impart.   12

Before you all your World, scaled beyond sight,
    However aided; beyond analogy
    With seeables; beyond the terms of light;   15

Both as to extent, incomprehensibly;
    And into micro-being, limitless;
    Bounded but by the mind's faint imagery,   18

Which, where it serves, has such persuasiveness
    We lend it what it needs, and let it mean,
    Though as to where it lead us we've no guess.   21

This is the imaginal curtain, the Veil between
    What's weaving it, O Muse, and what it hides.
    The simple do not know it for a screen;   24

Make it, our World, their god. Who so elides—
    So much it wavers—most of it will find
    Thrown out on the compost pile of deifieds,   27

Whence grow these leaves, these lines. For what's behind
    This strangest, most familiar thing we know,
    Toward that abyss—tasteless, scentless, blind,   30

Touchless, deaf, even wordless—we must go.
    Only in barest thought can we attain
    That which may teach us that the World's our Show.   33

Show so beyond conceiving that it's plain
    Men should be modest here and should resign
    Faint hopes, of thoroughly knowing it, as vain,   36

If *knowing's* what we've thought it, if we define
    Its ultimate as Becoming (Aquinas-wise)
    And make the rest cognizings we refine.   39

Thus the World's inexhaustible surprise:
    In beauty, foulness, horror, cruelty,
    In ecstasy and anguish . . . all that defies   42

Beyond

All our conjecture, tells us consummately
    To make with it what we may. (O Heavens, O Hell,
    We've made ourselves the last, most constantly.)   45

This *we*, here, is a betrayer—we may well
    Note and renounce. No man himself can conn.
    Few groups have had the chance or wit to dwell   48

Much as they would: on the Arawak fell the Don,
    Destroying them, for Spain-destroying gold,
    On Toussaint l'Ouverture, Napoleon.   51

Nor can new-model men be safe from old
    Till "servant-of-its-servants" Power grow
    And Man's Authority that Power hold.   54

Old-model men still rule: men picked as slow
    To guide their steps by Man's Authority,
    Accept it, and, at its command, forego   57

Their own demands, their groups'. Still enmity
    Their stock is. Deterrence their resort,
    As practical men, contemptuous of "The Key."   60

Yet Man's Authority springs from an OUGHT,
    Long overdue all lesser to control,
    An OUGHT that's now with Man's continuance fraught.   63

It has yet deeper sanction: within the whole
    He knows of now, there's nothing that can guide
    But this—that's no one's—all o'er-coming Soul: 66

Not Sciences only, Faculties beside:
    Affections, sentiments . . . left us, but entailed:
    A Legacy from men who may have died   69

To ensure it for Mankind. Thus we'll have failed
    If knowing it—*Become* it (Aquinas-wise)
    We serve it not, but let it be assailed.   72

Think clear: whence came each thought that through your eyes
 Helps them perceive whatever? By what innerved,
 Hangs all you apprehend beneath the skies?   75

That leaf you stroke, so curiously curved,
 Will you compare with leaves you can recall?
 Man has—all leaves with all. We are so served   78

That, Charity-led, even what must most appall
 In our own fiendish doings we can learn
 To count as illness truly and forestall.   81

Honour we then those who did so discern
 The cause of Evil; did so depose sad Hate,
 The Pathogen; did our joint effort turn   84

To serve in time—their genius our estate—
 What's left us of our World, did so redress
 Our hopes redeemed. May they reverse our Fate!   87

Forgive the voices saying this world is less
 Than what we live by: a Vale of Woe
 From which to look to other worlds—to bless   90

Or damn for ever. Let all such sick dreams go!
 They did Man's cause great hurt; became his curse;
 But helped him too to ask how we can know.   93

Failure inheres; what was thus for the worse
 May teach us still to watch all high intent.
 Hardly a curve we mold, a line of verse,   96

A plan we draw or a fine sentiment
 But covertly against its Source and Prince
 Can plot, nor show whereby it's bent.   99

Bent were our single minds, awry, long since;
 By Primal Fear wrenched ever more agley;
 Yet Man's Authority may, against all, evince   102

Beyond

Its straightening power. As triumphs Heaven's ray,
What Man now is—however old hopes wince—
Might, were we faithful, open for us a Way.   105

Commentary

I

The first four tercets are a proem introducing the prime contrast between the world view of 1300 and that from which these cantos come. This preface tries to recognize that what is said in *Whose Endless Jar* must still seem profanatory to many and even to its author as one brought up as a Christian. The other side to this is noted, too (ll. 9–11). A rebellious or at least controversial air is hard to preclude when positions so contrary are being compared. Yet animus in such a remonstrance as this would be an infection with the very complaint the verses profess to diagnose. Dante's world had no mercy on heretics; that was part of its derangement. Our counterview must beware—no longer of the old dangers but of new, among them a risk of frivolity.

Seer blest (l. 2). This loan from the *Ode on Intimations* does not accuse Dante of being childlike. But it can remind us of the prodigious differences there can be between poetic worlds—and of how differently the impulse to utterance can come to different spirits:

In the year that king Uzziah died I saw the Lord sitting upon a throne, high and lifted up, and his train filled the temple. Above him stood the seraphim: each one had six wings; with twain he covered his face, and with twain he covered his feet, and with twain he did fly. And one cried unto another, and said Holy, holy, holy, is the Lord of hosts: the whole earth is full of his glory. And the foundations of the thresholds were moved at the voice of him that cried, and the house was filled with smoke. Then said I, Woe is me! for I am undone; because I am a man of unclean lips, and I dwell in the midst of a people of unclean lips: for mine eyes have seen the King, the Lord of hosts. Then flew one of the seraphim unto me, having a live coal in his hand, which he had taken with the tongs

from off the altar: and he touched my mouth with it, and said,
Lo this hath touched thy lips; and thine iniquity is taken away, and
thy sin purged. And I heard the voice of the Lord saying, Whom
shall I send, and who will go for us? Then I said, Here am I; send
me. And he said, Go, and tell this people, Hear ye indeed, but
understand not; and see ye indeed, but perceive not. Make the
heart of this people fat, and make their ears heavy, and shut their
eyes; lest they see with their eyes, and hear with their ears, and
understand with their heart, and turn again, and be healed. Then
said I, Lord, how long? And he answered, Until cities be waste without
inhabitant, and houses without man, and the land become utterly
desolate, and the Lord have removed men far away, and the forsaken
places be many in the midst of the land.

—Isaiah 6:1–12

The morning on which Wordsworth dedicated himself to poetry:

> Magnificent
> The morning was, in memorable pomp,
> More glorious than I ever had beheld.
> The Sea was laughing at a distance; all
> The solid Mountains were as bright as clouds,
> Grain-tinctured, drench'd in empyrean light;
> And, in the meadows and the lower grounds,
> Was all the sweetness of a common dawn,
> Dews, vapours, and the melody of birds,
> And Labourers going forth into the fields.
>
> —*The Prelude* (1805–06) IV, 330–39

humour (l. 4). A medical use, as of choler or melancholy.

codes of rumour (l. 6). The systematic as well as the dubious
character of these apprehensions is remarked.

young a b c's (l. 8). The recency of many of the sources of
our contemporary world view is stressed. Developments are to
be expected.

from compliance (l. 12). Our provisionalities contrast with
certainties which may seem more inviting.

The verses then notice Dante's learning—in fields of study
strange to most of his present-day readers—and the scope of his

Beyond

design; also (with the fiercer passages of the Inferno in view) a malignancy easier to allow for if we bear in mind that he was sentenced to be burned alive if he returned to Florence.

Found Hatred (l. 20). Fate in the *Iliad,* and even in the *Republic,* is commonly autonomous. Homer's gods frequently intervene explicitly to prevent a hero from escaping his fate, as though that were something independent of them and above them, too. In Plato's myth of Er the returning souls choose their lots and can make stupid and careless mistakes in this. Each is given an attendant genius whose function it is to see that his lot befalls him. This enables the marshaling prophet to conclude his declaration of the word of the maiden, Lachesis, daughter of Necessity, with "Heaven is guiltless!" (*Republic* 617E). Dante's design, on the contrary, required that everything that happens be explained as the unquestionable (but incomprehensible) will of Heaven. The argument of my cantos is, in brief, that this makes Heaven very far from guiltless.

the deadly scheme (l. 21). Requital, penalty-reward (cf. II, 27). The central theme is here stated in the three following tercets. The madness (l. 1) (with the venom and rancors of the parenthetic ll. 16–18) is hatred—of which Hell is the expression and symbol. The task set, in opposition to that proposed in the *Comedy* (personal salvation), is the extirpation of this infective psychic cancer.

disdain (l. 22). Dante's *gran dispitto* (Inferno X, 36).

O still small voice (l. 24). I Kings 19:12–18: "And after the earthquake a fire; but the Lord was not in the fire: and after the fire a still small voice." (RV: *a voice of gentle stillness.*) It is worth remarking what this gentle voice says to Elijah upon Horeb, the mount of God—it commands vengeful slaughter. "And it shall come to pass that him that escapeth the sword of Hazael shall Jehu slay: and him that escapeth from the sword of Jehu shall Elisha slay." It may be added that this same voice is to say, through Hosea, "Yet a little while and I will avenge the blood of Jezreel upon the house of Jehu" (Hosea 1:4).

hear too late (1. 24). The findings of the most careful inquiries
into the human future do not indicate that we have much time
to spare. Under increasing pressures the danger that national
and group enmities will get out of control grows, too. These are
radically medical problems. As man's destructive capacity has
gone up, so, too, have his powers to devise and apply remedies.
But animosities of all sorts hold this back. Hatreds are patho-
logical but they are commonly thought meritorious.

A Source of Hate (1. 26). Those at the top who created Hell
(Inf. III, 5, 6) and through their agents conduct its operations.
We tend too easily to forget that the ultimate responsibility for
the police tortures, for example, which so disgrace our times,
lies with the governments that permit them. And other governments which do not protest and individuals, too, must share in
the disgrace.

Lines 31–45 have, as theme, the influence which conceptions
of their gods can have upon those who believe in them. That man
is made in the image of his God, and the converse, are both
propositions that can carry fearsome implications.

inexorable (1. 31). It is frequently reported that heads of states
let dislike and personal anger with one another guide policy.
The Old Testament, of course, is full of vindictive actions by
Jahveh.

Smithfield (1. 38). Where men of differing religious tenets
burned one another alive.

For sanction (1. 41). Persecutors have pleaded that their
severities might save dissentients from Hell.

that Great Soul's (1. 41). "Farinata, *magnanimo*" (Inf. X, 73).

So Worthy (1. 42). "Sì *degni*," Dante's earlier description of
Farinata in questioning Ciacco (Inf. VI, 79).

Three tercets (ll. 46–54) now comment on the image of
Lucifer, "*Lo imperador del doloroso regno*," "the Emperor of the
woeful realm," with which the hideousness of Hell comes to its
climax (Inf. XXXIV). The creature who was once so fair here
has three heads—somewhat as has that great effigy in the Ele-
phanta cavern, but with what other intent! His three faces—

one red, one black, one pale yellow—are so colored to represent the qualities of Impotence, Ignorance, Hate—opposites to the virtues of the three persons of the Trinity, virtues named in the inscription over the Gate of Hell: Divine Power, Supreme Wisdom, Primal Love. Lucifer fell through wishing to be as God, and has his wish here fulfilled. The degree of malicious mockery built into the description is superlative. Since Lucifer is, for that tradition, the first and worst of traitors, to his three mouths to chew eternally are given Judas Iscariot, Brutus, and Cassius, the three chief human traitors. His six eyes are endlessly weeping, his three chins dripping with tears and bloody foam. There is much more and, in all, it is a masterpiece, but what is its source?

strained cunning (l. 51). What does such an elaborate parody, contrived with such grim glee, tell us firstly about that which is being parodied and secondly about the poet who invented it? We are being told that this is what Power, Wisdom, and Love co-operate in doing when they fully exert themselves. Surely, since Treachery is the theme, we are justified in considering that such a representation is in itself no slight betrayal, made none the better for being perpetrated in the name of Justice (Inf. III, 4).

That worse betrayal far (l. 53). Blake's inscription on Drawing 101 of his illustrations to *The Divine Comedy* may be cited: "Whatever Book is for Vengeance for Sin and Whatever Book is Against the Forgiveness of Sins is not of the Father, but of Satan the Accuser and Father of Hell." And Crabb Robinson reports Blake as saying of the Supreme Being: "He is liable to error too— did he not repent him that he had made Nineveh?" And also: "*Dante* saw Devils, where I see none. I see only good." Another of Blake's notations (on design 7) is also relevant: "Everything in Dante's Commedia shows that for Tyrannical Purposes he has made This World the Foundation of All, and the Goddess Nature Mistress; Nature is his Inspirer and not the Holy Ghost." (See *Blake's Illustrations to the Divine Comedy,* by Albert S. Roe, to which I am here indebted.) As with his reading of the Book of Job, Blake's humane moral sensibilities, however obscure his mythology may be, are very evident.

Clearly, the concepts of justice appealed to and exemplified in the Inferno and those assumed in my verse comment could not be more apart. We are thus in a somewhat familiar situation—that in which Socrates was put, in Book II of the *Republic*—of being required to give a just account of justice.

It was a demand that he succeeded, consummately, in meeting. That having met it so well, the myth of Er was added, as a largely unconnected coda, reflects, I hope, not much more than Plato's awareness that a penalty-reward scheme satisfies deep, but certainly psychopathic cravings. Penalty as inducement may have some justification (though it has grave psychic dangers); penalty as retribution, no—whatever its appeal. Reward as inducement, similar drawbacks. Reward as compensation, as certainly, no. Decisions these, needed to protect the essential opposition of Right and Wrong. We are again, here, as we would expect, within a reflexive, self-applicable predicament. We are back, too, at the prime theme of Job.

If guilt there were (1. 60). The view these lines take is that guilt, if it should still be so regarded, attaches to all concerned, to all who have, in any degree, responsibility for wrong done. To make Satan or Eve uniquely faulty; to make war on Satan and use victory to punish him in this fashion (or to buy off Eve with the Christian sacrifice) would be, these verses hold, unjust. It would be damaging to Right and Wrong, as Ulysses put it in his superb oratorical display (*Troilus and Cressida* I, iii).

This great speech [5] has suffered for many diverse reasons: from being so dazzling as a set piece; from being the most extreme encomium in English of the virtues of rank and degree,

5. Rightly described by Reuben Brower as "the most eloquent and memorable expression in Shakespeare of the master idea inherited by his age from the medieval past—the belief in a grand scheme of an interrelated order in the cosmos, and in the individual life" in *Hero and Saint* (London: Oxford, 1971), p. 253. Brower's analysis of the speech deserves study phrase by phrase.

Beyond

the supreme anti-egalitarian declaration; from extolling all that
Thersites least respects and as coming from his "dog-fox Ulysses,"
who is moreover the head of the Greek Secret Service and can
praise it accordingly.

> There is a mystery—with whom relation
> Durst never meddle—in the soul of state,
> Which hath an operation more divine
> Than breath or pen can give expression to.

Such a claim naturally stirs contemporary hackles. But this speech
serves the better here and in what follows through uttering what
is so radically the view of the *Comedy* itself, for where else is
degree so celebrated but in the design of the Paradiso?

Ulysses, of course, addressing the "god-like seat" of "great
Agamemnon" is careful, in this grand consult, to keep the military
aim of his diagnosis in the forefront. He knows—as well even as
Homer's Odysseus—what he is doing. But for all his overt flattery,
"thy topless deputation" and so forth, the point and substance
and the solid ground of his speech is that Agamemnon is showing
himself to be incompetent. It is the Commander in Chief's duty
to see to it that subordinates understand what their duties are
and perform them. Then they, in their turn and place, can see
that their subordinates do so, too. If not, then necessarily:

> Strength should be lord of imbecility,
> And the rude son should strike his father dead:
> Force should be right; or rather, right and wrong—   116
> Between whose endless jar justice resides—
> Should lose their names, and so should justice too.
> Then every thing includes itself in power,
> Power into will, will into appetite;   120
> And appetite, a universal wolf,
> So doubly seconded with will and power,
> Must make perforce a universal prey,
> And last eat up himself. Great Agamemnon,
> This chaos, when degree is suffocate,   125
> Follows the choking.

And this neglection of degree it is
That by a pace goes backward, with a purpose
It hath to climb. The general's disdain'd   129
By him one step below, he by the next,
That next by him beneath; so every step,
Exampled by the first pace that is sick   132
Of his superior, grows to an envious fever
Of pale and bloodless emulation.

Ulysses might have concocted this matchless elucidation while elevated and inspired by a fresh and heady reading of the *Republic*. In soberer terms Shakespeare is here expounding the political theory which descends from Plato: the doctrine enunciating the fundamental conditions of sanity—for the state and for the individual alike.

The specialty of rule (l. 55). This is what "hath been neglected" (*Troilus and Cressida* I, iii, 78). It is degree. And how Shakespeare spells out, translates, explicates the *step* metaphor. From line 127 on he might be recounting just what Dante (and Milton, too, of course) is accepting from the tradition. Lucifer's strangely Achillean behavior is a response to a godlike Agamemnonic incompetence on Jahveh's side. "The general's disdained . . ." and so it goes on down from

> the first pace that is sick
> Of his superior . . .

(where *sick* may mean that something is going agley in Jahveh-Agamemnon, or that, as in modern colloquial, Lucifer-Achilles is disgusted with, fed up with, nauseated by his feckless and arrogant commander).

It is impossible to imagine a more penetrating analysis of a more important matter. We may note the exactness of the medical metaphors: the concepts of *sick* (both in the general sense of "ill . . . going wrong" and in the specific sense of "vomiting, reversal of right course,") recurring in *suffocate* and *choking*. In *suffocation:* "asphyxiation . . . not throbbing," failure of respiration, of due succession of expiration to inspiration. In *choking*, similarly, there is failure to follow in appropriate sequence. But what further goes wrong in Jahveh-Agamemnon? Instead of making sure that Lucifer-Achilles knows what his own duty is and thereby is enabled to do it, Jahveh-Agamemnon's line is precisely that "Strength should be lord of imbecility," and "Force should be right." He has not the faintest interest in understanding what Lucifer-Achilles' trouble is. He is merely an imbecile. The Almighty has the power but fails to see why he *must* not use it; he does not have the wisdom to see that, if he does so, in the end "Then every thing includes itself in power."

Ulysses might be taken as describing exactly the course of the traditional cosmos since the first stirrings of distrust and disaffection began in Lucifer. "By their fruits ye shall know them" has its appalling side. The fruit of elevating strength so (Thrasymachus-wise) has been to make it truly "lord of imbecility"—an imbecility exemplified perfectly by Dante's chewing Goblin. Through that primal error in making Force be right, it became inevitable that "right and wrong/Should lose their names and so should justice too."

Socrates' task in the *Republic* was to restore to these three their names, to show Plato's brothers and those they represent that justice is not "the interest of the stronger" and (a fortiori!) NOT the interest of the strongest. Unfortunately not even Plato could constantly remember and understand what Socrates had said to Crito in that prison dawn. (See ll. 86–88 below.) He forgot, and increasingly as the *Laws* drew out, that the primal wrong was the use of power in place of discernment. Many have, I suppose, wished to transfer the piercing lines (Inf. XXXIV, 34–36):

> S'ei fu sì bel com'egli è ora brutto,
> e contra 'l suo Fattore alzò le ciglia,
> ben dee da lui procedere ogni lutto.

> If he was once as beautiful as he is ugly now,
> and lifted up his brows against his maker,
> well may all affliction come from him.

from the horror there being depicted to another context. To what context perhaps a quotation from Plato, the mythmaker, may suggest (*Phaedrus* 249C):

This is a recollection of those things which our soul once beheld, when it journeyed with God . . . and therefore it is just that the mind of the philosopher only has wings, for he is always, as far as he is able, in communion through memory with those things communion with which causes God to be divine.

If the Highest lost communion with those things and replaced them with his will and power, well may he have become as hideous even as that contrivance of his at the bottom of his Hell.

My next ten lines (57–66) echo, transposing, some arguments from *Paradise Lost*. But *to seek, not passively await/Knowledge to come, withheld* (ll. 62–63) is from Paradiso XIX, 46–48:

> *E ciò fa certo che il primo superbo,*
> *che fu la somma d'ogni creatura,*
> *per non aspetta lume, cadde acerbo:*

And this is certified by that first proud being,
who was the summit of all creation,
because he would not wait for light, falling unripe:

"Good measures with itself and has no end" (l. 67). This is part of Dante's continuation from this tercet (XIX, 49–51):

> *e quinci appar ch'ogni minor natura*
> *e corto recettacolo a quel bene*
> *che non ha fino, e sè con sè misura.*

Hence it is apparent that each lesser nature
is a receptable too scant for that good
which has no end, and itself measures with itself.

Part of the meaning of this is that good (like justice, knowledge) is reflexive. We do not find something *else* in terms of which we can describe or appraise them. (This, however, is *not*, I think, to say that they are ʾindefinableʾ or, to turn this around, to say so would not be a useful way of using ʷindefinableʷ.)

Beyond

The next six lines derive from Dante's following passage (XIX). *the "Scripture over you"* (l. 73). Paradiso XIX, 83. The Just are still collectively (as that Eagle) instructing Dante. They are telling him that without what Scripture can teach him things might seem very unjust:

> *se la scrittura sopra voi non fosse*
> *da dubitar sarebbe a maraviglia.*

> were not the Scripture over you,
> there were marvellous ground for questioning.

This is a noteworthy admission, especially for those concerned with the corrupting lessons so much of the Bible has for so long so successfully taught to men.

We now return to Plato via Aristotle.

"True search for God is God's" . . . (ll. 76–78). "There are two ways only in which a science can be divine. . . . A science is divine if it is peculiarly the possession of God, or if it is concerned with divine matters. And this alone fulfills both these conditions" (Aristotle, *Metaphysics* A2, 983a).

All the Academy (l. 77). "Aristotle shares with him [the author of the *Epinomis*, that apocryphal conclusion to Plato's *Laws*], and with all Academics whatever, the view that *cognitio dei* is conceivable only if it is God Himself knowing Himself." [6]

And Aristotle's Plato taught (l. 79). In direct repudiation of what Achilles says to Priam (*Iliad* XXIV, 529). This rejection is discussed above. It may well be thought necessary for the protection of man's sanity. Not any God, but the defective Universe, now coming under our control, subjects us to evil.

And Plato's Socrates . . . (ll. 82–88). Crito has been urging Socrates to accept the means of escape from prison he can provide (*Crito* 49). Wrong done to any is here, for Socrates, damage done him. That this Key principle is described as so dividing those against and for it (these last, Socrates suggests, will be very few) is almost as striking as the statement of the

6. Werner Jaeger, *Aristotle* (London: Oxford, 1948), pp. 165–66.

Key position itself. History sadly confirms what Socrates expected without making the Key principle any the less crucial. (Cf. II, l. 84, and III, l. 60 below.)

one harrowed Hell (l. 89). See Inferno IV, 46–63.

But, in it, much . . . (ll. 91–92). "Then shall he say also unto them on the left hand, Depart from me, ye cursed, into everlasting fire, prepared for the devil and his angels"—Matthew 25:41. See also 13:40–42, 49, 50.

Bringing a sword (l. 93). Matthew 10:34. This may be saying in figurative language what Socrates said about his Key principle: that people of opposite opinions on "Resist not Evil" must despise one another. But, taken literally, how grimly true it has proved!

Love your enemies (l. 94). Matthew 5:44. The connection of this verse with 5:45 is a problem which exegetes have often prudently avoided. Both sunshine and rain are commonly beneficent; but both can be mercilessly destructive. And are we not to remember what eruptions and earthquakes can be like?

Forgive them (l. 95). In giving these references I am more than ever reminded of the enormous, disorienting-disoccidenting changes in possible readership that current writers on traditional themes must face. Sixty or fifty years ago, I could not have imagined that such pointers to these sources could be needed.

Hell's real Emperors (l. 99). Those named in the inscription over the Gate of Hell (Inf. III, 5, 6). The Divine Power, the Supreme Wisdom, the Primal Love—Father, Son, and Holy Ghost. That Hell is their work is the vast charge against the religion animating the *Commedia,* of which it is the highest epic utterance. This dogma is essential to the poem and is among its founding assumptions.

What we are we see (l. 100). "There is nothing behind the curtain other than that which is before it." See earlier discussion of the Hegel-Bradley position on appearances and reality in Chapter 5. See also lines 22–36 of Canto III below.

Beyond

find ourselves (l. 101). *"Mi ritrovai"* (Inf. I, 2). The varying interpretants offered by translators will show the richness of the meanings here: "I found myself"; "I came to myself"; "I was 'ware that I had strayed."

sifted so (l. 102). By our changing concerns, concernings, and discernments, traditionally from *cernere*, "to pass through a sieve," but Partridge regards this as a false reference.

the imperfect skies (l. 105). Recent indications are that many unimaginably remote galaxies are collapsing. For Dante's age the star world was the supreme visible exemplar of perfect order. This was so, too, for George Meredith's age.

> On a starred night Prince Lucifer uprose.
> Tired of his dark dominion, swung the fiend
> Above the rolling ball in cloud part screened,
> Where sinners hugged their specter of repose,
> Poor prey to his hot fit of pride were those.
> And now upon his western wing he leaned
> Now his huge bulk o'er Afric's sands careened,
> Now the black planet shadowed Arctic snows.
> Soaring through wider zones that pricked his scars
> With memory of old revolt from Awe,
> He reached a middle height, and at the stars,
> Which are the brain of heaven, he looked and sank.
> Around the ancient track marched, rank on rank,
> The armies of unalterable law.

No such certainties seem to be found in whatever imports the present-day cosmologies offer.

II

The first six tercets form an exordium. They ᴰbegin a webᴰ, select and set up a guiding pattern. In this instance, a highly familiar traditional comparison is used—that of the lives of individuals, in their successive generations, with the seasonal spring and fall of foliage. To recur to Dante's phrasing at the close of §XXV of *The Vita Nuova*, we will note that his image (as old as clothing, I suppose) of a "garb of figure," of which words can be divested, could mislead. For it is well recognized that the relation of figure and rhetorical color to the meanings that must be explained (the "true meaning" in question) is far closer and more essential than that of clothing to a body. This particular foliage metaphor—and this is the main reason why it is so old and accepted—has strong and clear implications. These constitute the web (texture, text) the exordium sets up. And the process of drawing explicit attention to these implications is here the exhibition of the "true meaning." In this figure a denial of an afterlife of any significance and of any punishment or reward are among them. We should add, perhaps, the compost heap's import. Leaf mold has its contribution. We may compare (from *Songs before Sunrise*, "The Pilgrims"):

> We men bring death lives by night to sow
> That men may reap and eat and live by day.

Swinburne's monosyllables put a parallel thought forcefully. This figure of Fall as necessary precondition of Spring is as firm and as universal as that by which dawn represents birth and nightfall death.

The pair of distichs I have used as epigraphs to the first two cantos may not call for glossing. I wonder how many who know them—in this or in variant forms—recall how they appear in Matthew 16:1–4:

1 The Pharisees also with the Sadducees came, and tempting desired him that he would show them a sign from heaven.
2 He answered them and said unto them, When it is evening, ye say, *It will be fair weather, for the sky is red.*
3 And in the morning: *It will be foul weather today for the sky is red and lowring.* O ye hypocrites, ye can discern the face of the sky, but can ye not discern the signs of the times?
4 A wicked and adulterous generation seeketh after a sign, and there shall be no sign be given unto it, but the sign of the prophet Jonas.

Beyond

Cf. Matthew 12:40:

For as Jonas was three days and three nights in the whale's belly; so shall the Son of man be three days and three nights in the heart of the earth.

The "heart of the earth" seems a strangely sinister way of describing Hell.

However, since green is here made much use of, its juxtaposition with its complementary, red, may deserve comment:

> Red in the morning:
> Shepherds' warning.

As green looks forward and is full of promise, so red is retrospective. Here it is the color of anger: that anger which, so near the beginning of time, created Hell: image to some, actuality to how many others, and portent of so much toil, trouble, and loss to those with flocks to care for.

> Red at night:
> Shepherds' delight.

Here red is no longer threatening or angry but charged with sunset. The end is near. The promise is for renewal in others.

"Rhetorical color" covers, of course, all the possible ways in which *how* anything is said affects *what* is said. Strictly, any change in the *how* affects (in some degree, small or great, produces change in) the *what*. Modern studies of what may be called the microsemantics of *poiesis* find that phonological and grammatical texturing as constantly convey rhetorical color as even etymological, figurative, or thematic interplay. The techniques of description through which this may be demonstrated are largely due to Roman Jakobson and such analyses might indeed be appropriately labeled Jakobsonian.[7] What these show,

---

7. For an example—one which could not possibly be more relevant to this entire discussion—see Roman Jakobson and Paolo Valesio, *Studi Danteschi*, vol. 43, "*Vocabulorum Constructio* in Dante's Sonnet '*Se vedi li occhi mici*,'" with special emphasis on syntactics. The virtue for which this sonnet prays is (though Dante will not agree) that for which this book is pleading.

above all, is the hitherto hardly suspected complexities of mutual support, qualification, modification, and opposition through which all features of the verbal vehicle co-operate in shaping and coloring the meanings of the utterance. An orderly collaboration and mutual control between *all* these levels has been revealed which would have very much astonished (could it have been shown them) the writers in whose lines this rises to its highest. To use the old iceberg image, that part of the work of composition consciously directed and performed by the poet is small in proportion to the orderings and organizings that are somehow *done for him* by skills about which he need consciously know little or nothing. If we take this as seriously as we now must, the degree of structure uncovered by a Jakobsonian analysis is so far beyond what would have been anticipated that the possible relations between verses and glosses to them have to be reconceived. There can be in the verses more meaning more delicately nuanced and more intricately composed than can be rendered in any gloss not inordinately long. Just to supply a Jakobsonian display will not do it. The display shows us how something is being done. It does not tell us what that something, that meaning, is—except in so far as it may help us to see that the meaning is commonly much less simple than we have supposed. And this can be extremely useful. Glosses, too, often suggest that they are telling us the meaning. They can tell us a part of it, but their real service should be in reminding us that there is probably an immense remainder, together with the occurrence of much in the verses that the writer may have been unaware of. That is what such studies can teach us.

In this case, the chief implications of the leaf-fall metaphor govern the canto throughout. A man's condition in Sheol is very like that of a fallen leaf, and the purgation at the close is the leaves' abandonment of their own prospects in the interest of the tree or, more fully, of the forest. The puns—with *leave* and with *leaf* as "page that is turned," and of *left*, "departed," and *left*, "remaining"—may be operative without being remarked. And the same is true of the recurrences of *l* and *f* (*left, leaves fall*, un*fur*l, *f*arewe*ll*, de*f*iant, reck*less*, *f*ailings, *F*it, He*ll*, and so on) throughout the exordium. I can vouch that neither the puns nor the phonologic patterning were in any way *planned* in the writing. They were, at most, unnoticed factors favoring certain words rather than others at choice-points, where *conscious* selection was concerned with and absorbed in, preoccupied by, quite other matters. Equally unwitting were the cyclic reversals (*l-f, f-l*), with their analogy to the round of the seasons. So, too, when the word *left* recurs (III, 86) and is followed by a return of the same *l-f, f-l* patterning: *Forgive, live, Vale, Failure*; in none of this was there any witting design.

leafit (l. 11). A Coleridgean word.

The interpretations offered for the Book of Job have been discussed above. My verses can seem to be far more confident of them than that prose treatment could be of any. So, too, with its sketch of Old Testament teaching.

calls the Omniscient's bluff (l. 44). Jung's amusement at the frequency with which Jahveh "fails to consult his omniscience" may be recalled.

grind the faces of the poor (l. 68) is Isaiah's phrase (Isa. 3:15), though Amos is the first from whom such denunciations are recorded, continuing till Amaziah, the priest of Bethel, sent unto Jeroboam saying, "The land is not able to bear all his words" (Amos 7:10).

Ardiaeos the Great (l. 84). See the *Republic*, 615C. Er, in the myth, reports of the afterlife, that he was within hearing when one was questioned by another: "Where is Ardiaeos the Great?" The other answered: "He has not come and probably he will never come. For this was one of the fearful things we saw. When we were near the mouth [of Hell] and were about to come out and all our pains were ended, we suddenly saw him . . . and the mouth would not let him through and roared against him. . . . And then violent men, like fire to look at, seized him and bound and flayed him, carrying him off to be thrown into Tartarus."

Eve's wish (l. 98). Both her Satan-inspired vision (*Par. Lost,*

V, 30–94) in slumber—which so strangely is forgotten and fails to warn her; one of Milton's most revealing insights—and her overweening conscious desire awakened by the Serpent.

III

The first four tercets, the invocation, have two duties: to reconcile, if they can, the audacity of the enterprise with the diffidence with which it must be approached. They try to do this in the traditional way by disowning responsibility, recalling how unaccountable are sources of any utterance, of all enterprise indeed. They remind, too, by the instances they cite, of how much in what is now shaping man's incalculable future has always seemed impossible but has now been swiftly accomplished—even within the span of one lifetime.

With those confining Logic, with Niels Bohr (l. 5). Gödel's Theorem, for example, limiting the scope of proof. It is not, perhaps, yet clear how much Logic's own recognition of its shrunken power enlarges man's; but Bohr's Principle of Complementarity (*Dialectica* I, 315) has helped—beyond any previous dreams—to free physicists' inquiries. Bohr was not sure how far similar freedoms should be taken in other fields. Only trying them out can tell us. This book can be regarded as an attempt to try some of them out.

Their soil, this page (l. 12). The line looks forward to ll. 76–78, and back to the last line of Canto II.

This is the imaginal curtain (l. 22). I may here transcribe the lines from Hegel's *Phenomenology of Mind* to which F. H. Bradley seems to be referring in the passage discussed in Chapter 5 above. "It is manifest that behind the so-called curtain, which is to hide the inner world, there is nothing to be seen unless we ourselves go behind there, as much in order that we may thereby see, as that there may be something behind there which can be seen." [8] How huge the differences between what Hegel said and what Bradley conceived!

8. J. B. Baillie, trans. (New York: Humanities Press, 1964), p. 212.

on the Arawak fell the Don (l. 49). Samuel Eliot Morison reports: "Las Casas, who spent the better part of a noble life vainly invoking the words and example of Jesus against the cruel and inordinate greed of Castilian Christians, comments . . . in stern and measured words: 'Note here, that the natural, simple and kind gentleness and humble condition of the Indians, and want of arms or protection, gave the Spaniards the insolence to hold them of little account, and to impose on them the harshest tasks they could, and to become glutted with oppression and destruction.' " [9] He records further: "The policy and acts of Columbus for which he alone was responsible began the depopulation of the terrestrial paradise that was Hispaniola in 1492. Of the original natives, estimated by a modern ethnologist at 300,000 in number, one third were killed off between 1494 and 1496. By 1508 an enumeration showed only 60,000 alive. Four years later that number was reduced by two thirds; and in 1548 Oviedo doubted whether 500 Indians remained." [10]

On Toussaint l'Ouverture, Napoleon (l. 51). The first and probably the ablest of great black liberators (1743–1803) equal, most likely, in genius, resource, and energies to his opponent, Toussaint did miraculous things for Saint-Domingue—the present Haiti—then overwhelmingly France's most providing colony. He liberated its slaves and somehow almost re-established its prosperity. But then the incensed Corsican, who wished to reimpose slavery and had dreams of seizing Eastern America for France, launched the largest expeditionary force that has yet crossed the Atlantic from East to West. It failed; but when the French were collapsing, Toussaint was trapped, treacherously, and carried off to the Fort de Joux in the Jura ("little better than an inhabited block of ice"). Here he was harshly treated—by order of Napoleon, who believed that Toussaint had great wealth stowed away somewhere. But Toussaint had paid his soldiers with it. Within a year, in a cell "little better

9. *Historia de las Indias*, quoted in *Admiral of the Ocean Sea, A Life of Christopher Columbus* (Boston: Little, 1946), p. 291.
10. Ibid., p. 493.

The Divine Comedy

than a trench" and with hardly any outlook, this great man died (April 6). I append (I have followed Wordsworth's spelling of l'Ouverture) the sonnet published in *The Morning Post,* Feb. 2, 1803, two months before.

TO TOUSSAINT L'OUVERTURE

Toussaint, the most unhappy man of men!
Whether the whistling Rustic tend his plough
Within thy hearing, or thy head be now
Pillowed in some deep dungeon's earless den;—
O miserable Chieftain! where and when
Wilt thou find patience! Yet die not; do thou
Wear rather in thy bonds a cheerful brow:
Though fallen thyself, never to rise again,
Live, and take comfort. Thou has left behind
Powers that will work for thee; air, earth, and skies;
There's not a breathing of the common wind
That will forget thee; thou hast great allies;
Thy friends are exultations, agonies,
And love, and man's unconquerable mind.

"servant of its servants" (l. 53). One of the Pope's titles is *servus servorum.*

Man's Authority (l. 54). Wisdom.

"The Key" (l. 60). This looks back to I, 84 and II, 84.

Not Sciences only (l. 67). From Donne's *The Exstasie:*

> So must pure lovers' soules descend
> T'affections and to faculties
> Which sense may reach and apprehend
> Else a great Prince in prison lies.

See my discussion of the stanza in *Poetries: Their Media and Ends* and in my "Complementary Complementarities," in *Internal Colloquies.*

—Become it (Aquinas-wise) (l. 71). Coleridge called genuine knowledge "that which returns again *as power.*" That with and through which we truly think, feel, know, act is *something we have become* or (we might equally say) *something that has*

Beyond

become us. The verses return here to I, 69 and III, 37. Dante uses superlatively simple and vivid terms for such interpenetrations and mutualities (Par. IX, 73):

Dio vede tutto, e tuo veder s'inluia,
  diss' io, beato spirto, sì che nulla
voglia di sè a te puete esser fuia.

"God seeth all, and into him thy seeing sinketh" (in-hims itself)
  said I, "blessed spirit, so that no wish
  may steal itself from thee."

And again (Par. IX, 80–81):

Gia non attenderei io tua domanda
s'io m'intuassi, come tu t'immii

Not till now had I awaited thy demand
  Were I in thee even as thou art in me.
  (if I in-thee myself as thou thyself in-me'est)

Think clear . . . (ll. 73–75). Illusions of independence often hide from us that only through what we have learned from others can we do or be anything. As in the diagram of the Divided Line in the *Republic* (509–11), all the hierarchies of apprehensions ultimately depend from the Idea of the Good, so all an individual's capacities are enabled by the strivings—seekings for the good, well-directed or mistaken, sane or sick—of others.

That leaf you stroke (l. 76). The central image of Canto II returns. Whether or not this leaf is here a life, a someone, the verses take botany as exemplar or type specimen of man's wisdom, power, and love. This is something quite beyond any one individual's ability to compass. In place of botany we may think of what the leaves of the ideal Dictionary hold. How often our choice of a word, thought, or resolve is but a reminding communication from an etymon!

May they reverse our Fate (l. 87). The tercet links with I, 24; II, 70, and III, 85–87.

The last four tercets begin by echoing the last lines of Canto

150

The Divine Comedy

I. They glance again (l. 98) at Donne's "great Prince," and end with a recognition (in accord with the close of the Inferno) that treachery is our worst ill: the deadliest infirmity that Man is heir to.

The very elaboration with which Dante utters his hatred (God's Hatred) of Satan, as Traitor, and the means he used to make his image as ugly, as hideous, as hateful as can be—as inverse as possible to the images beyond imagining with which in Paradiso he draws towards its close—approach the limits of language. No one was ever so good as Dante at saying "Words fail" while managing to make them do more than seems conceivable. Yet in the end—for both his polar opposites—what he can give us is only an aid: "the god when conceived is not the reality"; the imaginal curtain has not been drawn aside.

At the supreme Shinto shrine at Ise, a white silk veil hangs shimmering. It and its supporting frame are constantly renewed to seem ever pristine and not of the world. To this, so it is told, came no less than a modern minister of education, who leaned forward to lift a corner of the curtain with the ferule of his walking stick. He died by a zealot's knife before he reached his home.

His was an idle curiosity—indulged through a failure of due reverence, an inadequacy of imagination. He should have known that there would be nothing behind the veil worth seeing at the price of the mistreatment of such a symbol.

Dante's curtain, unlike the veil at Ise, is as highly figured as any texture can be. It must be so to meet his "practical end . . . to remove those who are living in this life from the state of wretchedness and lead them to the state of blessedness" (*Letter to Can Grande*, 267–70). In brief, to bring home the vision of our life's journey he would have us see. The Ise veil, in contrast, presents merely the reminder that what we see is still a veil. The cartoon-figured curtain that my verses have hung up is in between: as far from Dante's intense actualities as from the purities of the Shinto shrine. Mine has holes in it

151

through which educators can readily peek. And it shows all sorts of signs of how it has been composed. These, however, are all part of it. Being explicitly a reminder of imperfection, it tries, like the philosophers of the *Phaedrus,* to remember, too, its loyalty towards that from which *im*perfections depart: "that through communion with which the god-like is divine." Its concern with loyalty therefore is more Socratic than Dantean.

So the treachery is not there located in (assigned to) the Seraph Lucifer who "lifted up his brows against his Maker" (Inf. XXXIV, 35); rather, it is found in (charged against) that Maker (to suppose 'It-Him' such). Satan-Lucifer's adverse gesture (whether defiant—a tilting up of the whole head—or merely quizzical—the raising of an eyebrow) was in this alternative representation met by swift violence. And this violence in place of the elucidation that Lucifer's name invited was, it is suggested, the original treachery to the professed designed order. This was the break, the fault, the failing, the faithlessness, the infidelity, from which so much sorrow has ensued. But these words here are too harsh, too uncharitable. For, as in so many of its reverberations, resort to violence rather than to instruction (to further attempts to inform) suggests a weakness, a helplessness, a lack of more adequate resource with which in men's governmental activities we are all too familiar. To replace, as my verses do, the old traditional myth of Satan's Revolt as the original Wrongdoing calling for the original Requital (the original act of retributive justice) by an inverse myth—that of a rough, hot-tempered, malicious use of punishment instead of reason—may, to some, still seem merely whimsical or perverse. But to others—and increasingly—this inversion and transformation of attitudes has now become nothing less than our only hope. New School Elucidation as against Old School Violence: that is the choice. The Old School setup is now too military, too exterminatorial, to be anything but suicidal. Its partisans are long overdue to be converted.

I have deliberately used mild, old-fashioned terms: *rough, hot-tempered, malicious* are hardly suitable expressions with which to describe, say, the Vietnam bombings or the electronic warfare there being developed for application elsewhere. Our powers to do *wrong* along with our ruthlessness in using them have recently increased beyond all measure. So, too, have *our powers to do right*—if only we would consider more carefully what we *should* instead be doing. As man's capabilities in destruction and instruction increase together, the fact that violence is inherently pernicious ("the way of death," see Dictionary) and enlightenment inherently salutary (ᴰconducive to safety and healthᴰ) becomes more evident—though not widely, rapidly, deeply, and effectively enough. Hence these pages. But neither the relocation of the ⁿᵇfaultⁿᵇ this inverse myth represents nor the remedy it indicates is new. Satan-Lucifer's analogies with Prometheus are signs of perception that can call on the very Dictionary as witness. To take only the first page of *Webster's Collegiate* and the most suggestive words there treated:

The first and smallest of these, *a,* is also the most interesting with its extraordinary variety of contributions to our handling of meanings.

a, as indefinite article, abbreviation from *an,* "1. One; some particular; one kind of. 2. Any, each; the same. 3. [Deriv. fr. AS. *an, on.*] In, to, or for each." Already the interplay, the challenge to choose among these, within each and between the three, is high. But, as the prefixes that follow are compared, our feeling that *a, a-* can be almost anything, many times simultaneously, is confirmed. *a,* prep. meaning "of." *a* as 3 above meaning "in," "on," "at." *a* as intensive: "arise." *a* as "from off." *a* as reduced *ad* meaning "to." *a* as meaning "not." And lastly *alpha privative,* from Greek *an, a* denoting "less," "not," "without," "un." There is an extraordinary object lesson here in how a (any) part of a sentence takes (or should take) its force—the kind and degree of its contribution to the work of the whole—from the rest of that whole. There is thus within any sentence using any of the above meanings, a micro-but-quintessential dramatic action by which the resources of *a* are put at the disposal of one or other or several or all of the aims of the utterance. I need not point out how this minim but ever-recurrent playlet parallels the protocosmic drama we have been examining. Lucifer—ranking A1 among Seraphs—being as yet insufficiently enlightened about his duty, needed help (Par. XIX, 46–48) and instead of that got Hell for it: whence our woe. That Dante wrote *cadde acerbo*, "falling *un*ripe," is strangely suggestive. For a moment he is taking a diagnostic interest: Lucifer should have waited; in due time would some process of growth and development have improved this 'summit of all creation' and equipped him for even higher duties than those of leader of the archangels? Then, we may suppose, there would have been no occasion for any Fall. Instead, he "fell unripe."

Mercilessly punished—the sadly jejune *Gospel of Bartholomew* says that he and his angels were "senseless for forty years" from the shock of their casting down—he renews, via Eve, his still-continuing revenge for his ill-treatment. While we are on such time aspects, we may recall that Dante is told by Beatrice (Par. XXIX, 49–51) that the rebellious angels fell—"did disturb the substrate of your elements"—in less time than it takes to count to twenty.

Our other select words from *Webster's Collegiate*, page 1, continue the commentary: *aback* [D]surprised, checked, disconcerted[D]; *Abaddon*, the [D]destruction, the place of the lost in Sheol[D]; *abandon* [D]from jurisdiction, to give (oneself) up without attempt at self-control, banish, expel, a yielding to natural impulses[D]; *abase* [D]lower, depress, hurl down, to cast down, reduce in rank, office, estimation, etc., degrade[D]. If we keep the confrontation of the Almighty and Lucifer in mind, such words, as we pursue their possible meanings, will seem to be talking of that primal cataclysm above all. And if, as we should, we let the Dictionary send us, by cross-reference or without it, to the Dictionary, we will find *disconcert* (with *discompose* and *concert*) yet further developing the theme. Or, if you will, preaching the same sermon, stating the case from both sides—though with startling changes in the values of the principal terms.

The Divine Comedy

So much for a sample of what the Dictionary—the oldest living depository and record of thought—can show us as to the origin of evil. We may usefully supplement such lessons with what one of the newer of the sciences of the creative process can tell us. If we look up *fault* in the *Collegiate* we are given a very helpful diagram illustrating what Man's Authority in geology can offer us towards understanding (and possibly preventing and remedying, or at least mitigating, by foresight) some of the most terrible disasters the biosphere is liable to.

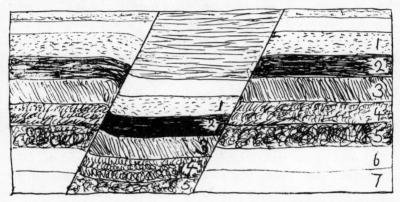

With any type-specimen display of exposed strata—the Grand Canyon, for example—to look at, it is not difficult for anyone to imagine and realize what strains and tensions Earth's shrinkage must produce. Something has to give and when it does suddenly, we know what happens. "Sermons in stones" indeed: for *As You Like It,* read together with *Troilus and Cressida* (*As You Don't Like It*), can seem in passage after passage the gayest, most brave and gallant complement to Ulysses' "tale of length." Degree being vizarded,

> What plagues, and what portents, what mutiny,
> What raging of the sea, shaking of earth,
> Commotion in the winds, frights, changes, horrors,
> Divert and crack, rend and deracinate
> The unity and married calm of states
> Quite from their fixure!

Ulysses throughout his depiction might be having this very diagram before his mind's eye. And Jaques' most provocative line: "Ducdame, ducdame, ducdame," with his gloss on it: "'Tis a Greek invocation to call fools into a circle" (II, 5, 59), can, for those who read it with the rest of the play livingly in mind, be taken as inviting us to ponder both the reflexive, self-applying character of our central positions discussed above and sophrosyne as being the unity and married calm of states in which disturbances, endless jars, were so constantly (inevitably) Shakespeare's prime concern. The two plays together form a comment on the paradox that order, degree, government derive equally from that which should be governed and from that which should govern. Any violence hurts the whole. It was with this in view that those of the Old School of government were described above as partisans—a word associated with appeal to and threat of violence.

I have not been as far from Dante in all this as may seem. The point to be made has been that the God-Devil, Heaven-Hell oppositions the *Comedy* uses are oversimple and, in view of present and future human powers, far too dangerous to be allowed much influence any longer. A new order of accommodation and mutual study between holders of contending positions will be required if the Tertiary Period is not soon to be ended by the mistakes of man.

We may then well once again consider how extensions of the Principle of Complementarity can serve to mitigate or even avoid clashes between those who do and those who do not find Luciferian co-operation necessary. Those belonging exclusively to either party will, of course, point out at once that in physics incompatible rival hypotheses may well be jointly useful but that in morals and religion this cannot be so: integrity requires exposure and rejection of error. As this position is stated, with any of the firmness that a clear consciousness of virtue inspires, we will feel that we are back with Socrates in his prison, sadly foreseeing that few will ever accept his Key principle and that those of opposite views must despise one another. But, with

Shakespeare's aid, can we not see that a high enough concept of the order to which we must be loyal makes any such contempt itself a betrayal? Right and Wrong must not lose their names; *within* every view there will and must still be error and defect. But—complementarians may suggest—conflicting views may nonetheless be mutually serviceable and indeed indispensable. In brief, account must be taken of the conditions under which the views arise, of the standpoints and of the aims each standpoint serves. An adequate geometry of possible standpoints and purposes, I have tried to show, is our ever-increasing need. Only that can keep conflicting views from trespass. Evidently this goes back to the concept of justice outlined in the *Republic:* let every view do its work (as well as it can) and let it not interfere with the work that other views have to do. The duties of the Guardians would fall upon the interpreters of the Complementarity Principle, who would have to rule upon and prevent trespass.

Socrates laughs at Glaucon for oversimply supposing that the course of studies he is sketching for the Guardians is anything more than a bare prelude or introduction. Palpably so, too, here. To distinguish our purposes and discern which views advance which aims is not less than the whole duty of man. It is another way of describing the task of forming a just concept of justice. And it brings us around again to the fourth sentence in my first paragraph above on the *Comedy.* In what position are we now to comment on whether the poem is in fact judging of any world but its own, and on whether Requital is in *any* world—even in that now, at last, vanishing Christian world— a morally redeemable misconception?

On the first point our Guardian interpreters would, I think, recommend the view that this poem (as with any other) can only be judged justly by itself. It has set up—by the mode in which it has come to be—its own problem and conditions, and what it may do, being thus circumscribed, is its own business. It is autonomous, self-governing. But this does not imply either that it cannot trespass or that what it does, within its own jurisdiction, may not be wrong. And, in fact, it has trespassed. It has done so through the Christianity it represents—probably the most aggressive major cultural organization ever known, ready at times to use any means to further its ends. We may reflect further that Christianity has been thus aggressive because it has been powered by such a theology.

Whether within the poem the Requital concept is wrong, damaging to the poem itself, is not so easy to determine. It is centrally necessary to the *Comedy*, which could not be itself without it. What the poem does through and only through the concept might be held to be its sufficient justification. Outside the poem—in the other worlds of which the poem has been held to judge—the Requital concept *is* wrong. It is an ancient, still frequent, and still powerful malformation of the mind, a misconception dangerous in itself and obstructive to wiser treatment of many grave ills. But within the poem what it makes possible may be enough insulation, strong enough to keep it from injuring the rest. The ragings in Heaven (for example, the thunder cry at the end of Par. XXI) may raise a doubt: vengeance conflicts with too much else there. Perhaps those internal conflicts, and the unique values of that else, might serve as a sort of cordon guarding neighbor worlds from infection.

7

The Scripture over You

Or tu chi sei, che vuoi sedere a scranna
per giudicar da lungi mille miglia
con la veduta corta d' una spanna?

Certo a colui che meco s' assottiglia,
se la scrittura sopra voi non fosse,
da dubitar sarebbe a maraviglia.

Now who art thou who wouldst sit upon the seat
to judge at a thousand miles away with the
short sight that carries but a span?

Truly to him who goeth subtly to work with me,
were not the Scripture over you, there
were marvellous ground for questioning.
                                    —Il Paradiso XIX, 79–84

As with that central type specimen, sameness-difference, which
figured in the Prologue, three or more (Nominalist, Realist,
Conceptualist) modes of approach, though mutually exclusive
and no one of them in any sense 'solving' the problem, could
be mutually helpful, so with most (possibly all) of the key

159

concepts the intervening chapters have been presenting. Not any 'answer' but further insight, more depth and clarity in the questioning has been all the discussion has aspired to. (It might be mentioned in passing that sometimes the choice of one semantic marker rather than another has been really a decision about one or other compacted philosophy the marked term might be bringing in.)

Judge not, that ye be not judged (Matt. 7:1), the most reforming of all enjoinders, has its most searching application here. While we might (or must) seem to be judging the *Iliad,* the *Republic,* the tale or poem of Job, and *The Divine Comedy,* that is an appearance, no more. What is being judged is the ability, the resources: the outer and inner testimony being called upon. And as we inquire into and attempt to assess *these,* bringing in other investigations to qualify what might seem straighter questions about the *Iliad* or the Book of Job, do we not find ourselves required to recognize that, in all cases, a number of alternative, mutually exclusive viewpoints or positions are not so much in competition as contributary?

(Here conscious, explicit use will be made of this essential metaphor, waking it up and inviting it to become as active and participatory as it can. For anyone hoping to *see* what anyone means, or to have what he himself means taken aright, the viewpoint image is the most serviceable of all: an instance wonderfully and efficiently representing all that it can exemplify; the geometrical conditions of an aspect standing for *any conditions whatsoever* of any presentation.)

Such an unusual emphasis may be justified by the help a clear remembrance of our viewpoint situation might be in guarding ourselves from one of the most persistent of the infections the intellect is liable to: forgetting a necessary limit to what it can attempt to do. After absorbing, as best we can, the conjoint influences of a variety of positions, the notion or assumption that there must be some *one* position privileged to yield the *one* true, the *one* right, the only correct and valid view, is weakened. This notion has, however, the qualities of an invasive weed and is excessively hard to eradicate. The soil condition which invites and protects it is the indicative mood. My use of this in this appeal—hard to avoid—risks reintroducing the very notion I would expel.

A caveat is clearly needed here. Too often an acceptance of this "multiple-viewpoint" position is accompanied by a vague notion (as weedlike as the other) that any view thus becomes somehow as good as any other. Nothing could be sillier, or less accordant with the exacting selections a reflective multiple-viewpoint position requires. Any view whatsoever may be, in itself and apart from other views, valid internally or invalid: sufficiently clear and just in its own right or defective, whether corrigible or not, blurred, or impaired in countless ways. The multiple-viewpoint position asks us, pre-eminently and particularly, to remember this. Commonly, indeed, defects in a view are shown up by the co-operating other views—in fashions unrealizable if the defective view were taken to be uniquely right.

Perhaps the saddest and most humbling thing about the later history of man—since religions and ideologies took to dreaming of world conquest—has been the combination, on such a scale, of the worst defects in views with the uttermost conviction of unique validity. Poor misguided faith has been so frequently and widely exalted into Prince of Virtues. No hospital for the insane is without its varied examples, piteous and terrible, of this conjunction of diseased view with diseased conviction. What is more pitiable and daunting still is the historic record of the extent to which similar perversions have been set forth as keys to salvation; often with fiercest penalties for those unsuccessful in conniving. There are conditions, we should remember, when insane and criminally pernicious doctrine can do anything. How soon will climbing rulers and their followings have entirely forgotten Hitler?

A multiple-viewpoint position would aim to protect us from such aberrations by encouraging in all (and we have the technological means to do so) the entertainment of as full and round a variety of views as we can compass, together with as much shrewd clarification of each view as we can undertake. Above all, mutual charity among conflicting views is this over-all position's own governing condition. No dictatorship then, but—in each mind's Republic—rather a Blakean State in which each component lives by co-operating with each of its fellows,

> Pitying and forgiving all
> Our transgressions great and small,

collaborating (much as the nervous system does) in a comprehension of how and why each must fall short, and as to what to do about it then. A model, this, for the individual and not inappropriate, as Plato saw it, for the state—which for us, today, is not a dream of Athens but of a viable, continuable World Order.

It was not without premonition of these dangers that Niels Bohr pressed for the recognition in more complex studies (such as those with which these chapters have been concerned) of his Complementarity Principle, made so evident by the situation in atomic physics. There the very simplicity of the transactions under study made it manifest that experimental-conceptual setups which are *mutually exclusive* (his favorite term), as with particle and wave transmission, could yet yield results valuable in further inquiries. He rightly insisted that the extension of this principle into other and immeasurably more complex fields—into psychology, metaphysics, and what we now call semantics—is no matter of inventing "more or less vague analogies," but of seeing in the more complex inquiry the same inescapable fact that had become so obvious in physics: every investigation depends upon, is limited and shaped by the instruments through which it is made possible and conducted. The most important, of course, of these instruments are our concepts. And in these more complex inquiries we may especially bear in mind that a concept (as its etymon and cognates indicate) is a descendant and that its heredity may have consequences. What we have been concerned with in this book is the heredity of some of our chief concepts.

The Scripture over You

It will not be surprising if, as genetics and semantics develop, their mutual relevances grow more apparent.

Concepts, however, though no doubt the most important, are not our only mental tools; nor are they ordinarily or often independent of the other means through which we manage our thinking and our lives. It is indeed more than a little odd that we habitually regard thoughts as just thoughts—not bothering much to consider in any detail how they may be related to the other components of our mental process. I will not attempt here any such account—having done so often enough.[1] I will remark only that the viewpoints we are concerned with differ cognitively (referentially), imaginally, valuatively, conatively, *and* in selective, animating purpose. We can hardly expect communications and collaborations to improve (except in strictly technological fields) unless means are found to make the co-operations between the components of our meanings more examinable and amenable to control. It is through malfunction here that miscomprehensions and frustrations, between as well as within minds, chiefly arise.

As I write my eye has happened upon a sentence in an admirable article: "Most people's lives are questionable documents in which illusion and fact are interchangeable, in which love and status, say, as in the case of Swann, may be real personal and social powers but—from a viewpoint only one turn of the screw away—also ridiculous shams."[2] One turn of the screw away: slight the shift in position, vast the consequences. Whether in due course we may become at all able to describe or plot these displacements systematically, only the event can show. In thousands of ways—automatic, instinctive, traditional, invented *ad hoc*, improvised—we are forever trying "to see how it might look from another angle." It may be premature to try to devise *methodical* means of comparing these transitions; but physical naviga-

1. Principally in *Speculative Instruments* (Chicago: Univ. of Chicago Press, 1955; New York: Harcourt, Harvest Books, 1967), pp. 17–38.
2. Geoffrey Moss, "One Hundred Years of Proust," *The New Yorker,* 18 December, 1971, p. 130.

Beyond

tion, too, was once a hunchy, at best hit-or-miss business—more often miss than hit.

In the absence of an adequate methodical procedure for comparing views (with due reference to their viewpoints), we might do best to consider not viewpoints "only one turn of the screw" from one another, but viewpoints extremely opposed; cases where we might catch ourselves muttering "one hundred eighty degrees"—the viewing minds being eye-to-eye or back-to-back. (We will probably find that eye-to-eye confrontations commonly involve not a little back-to-back outlooking.) The foregoing discussions have presented many such situations: the Platonic-Homeric, Socratic-Achillean antagonisms, those between Job and his comforters (and between Jahveh and Shaddai), and that which raises the crucial problem—Requital—with *The Divine Comedy*. This last: the status of reward and punishment in a moral outlook is the most challenging. It might, if warily explored, enable the contemporary revolt against Christianity to be represented as a set of comparable—and perhaps mutually comprehensible, not reprehensible—viewpoints.

Imaginative vehicles, from the *Rig Veda* or the *Iliad* through *The Divine Comedy, Paradise Lost,* and *Prometheus Unbound,* have always been the most powerful, versatile, unruly, and miscellaneously effective of theological influences. They have seized and held minds as have no other vehicles—even when allowing of almost any interpretants. And they have been able to do this for extraordinarily varied readers. The narratives of the Bible have been, of course, the prime examples. They have, as regards their interpretations, been under the guardianship of the most organized and fanatical bodies of exegetes known. Largely for this reason divergencies in readings have resulted in the most disgraceful persecutions and exterminations known until we come to those of our own century. If philosophies *are,* "next to parlour games and spring millinary, the most fugacious of human toys" (as "Q" once remarked), we must equally agree that theologic doctrines—when imaginatively conveyed and charged, as so often, with philosophic potentials—have been the most dangerous of man's many inventions. No powers without their perils. This is evidently also an indication of how and why imaginative vehicles can also be, under other conditions, what Shelley hoped they were in *Defence of Poetry.*

We too often behave as though we should suppose that "imaginative" is necessarily a term of praise; and not since Locke's day has "poetic" been widely used for disparagement. This belongs to the still criminally neglected topic of bad art (Hitler) and of the destructive uses of good art. Granting that both words normally carry strong laudatory suasions and implications, we can, in analysis, usefully set these aside to consider how its imaginative structure in a vehicle (way of saying something) can increase the powers, for good or evil, of its tenor (what it is taken to be saying). In such instances as we have here in mind —the accounts of God's dealings with man, and particularly with Israel, that dominate the Old Testament (the Book of Job being the great exception); the link via Messianic prophecy with the New; the climax of the Crucifixion and its aftermath; and the Apocalypse, as horrific coda—their flexibility—the fact that almost every verse (from early days so called; furrows in that enormous field, indeed) can be and has been read both literally, in varying senses, and symbolically (metaphorically) in a hardly conceivable range of differing fashions—this (and, of course, the depth of the concern they engage) is what gives such vehicles their prodigious power. Coleridge in his last years urging that the Bible be read symbolically as well as literally was a little ahead of his contemporaries but hardly enough. He was aware of only the first waves from the applications, in Germany, of the understanding to the textual complexities and the variety of the outer testimony as to how the Bible had been read. That he, of all men, should not have seen more deeply into what was oncoming, further shows the strength of the Bible's hold. As Walter Jackson Bate shrewdly remarks: ". . . in this he led the way for later generations of Englishmen, who, staggered by the results of historical

Beyond

and textual study of the Bible, hurried into the storm shelter that Coleridge had already provided." [3] It was not to remain any sort of shelter for long. By the time of Matthew Arnold's *Literature and Dogma,* the literal reading was, for the apprised, precariously conjectural throughout, and symbolic readings (as knowledge of the outer testimony developed) were turning into a welter irresponsible enough to make any conscientious inner testimony doubt itself. As Arnold had it: "Our religion . . . has attached itself to the fact" (but when had it not?), "and now the fact is failing it." He could still hold, however, to symbolic reading. "But for poetry the idea is everything." The 'idea', which thus stands over against the fact, being a symbolic as opposed to a literal tenor.

Such perturbations were, however, only for the sufficiently informed and self-examining reader, the critically alerted student. The vast majority of readers, looking rather for guidance and support than for satisfactory assurance, and, in most cases, without any hermeneutic standards whatsoever, read as before. On them the power of the Bible, speaking with unique authority of their deepest concerns, remained relatively untroubled and undiminished. It still nourished the questionings which it had itself implanted. The cultural continuity was sufficiently maintained. It could prevent—and to some degree still does—other questionings about its own fitness as guide and support for moral effort, as model for conduct. And as to any probable effects upon behavior of a devout acceptance of what it had presented, such questionings were barely as yet on the horizon. Now that we have to doubt, as very few a century ago could, whether the politico-industrial interferences of Judean-Christian enterprise with the rest of mankind have been as desirable as was supposed, we may well bear in mind that the Bible has been the educator of the West far longer and far more deeply than Homer had been "the educator of Greece" when Plato so described him. Plato had the freedom and the courage to depose Homer and to give

3. *Coleridge* (New York: Macmillan, 1968), p. 223.

explicit reasons why neither the Olympians nor Achilles were worthy models.

At the end of Chapter 2 above, there is a suggestion that we should consider what the vision of the heroic created by the *Iliad* has done and might still do to man. The most dangerous of the influences, those that have cost us the most, are not those that led to Plato's revolt. They are best seen today as embodied in the ideals of nationalism. Relatively few individuals—though, from another point of view, far too many—think of themselves as Achilles did: as a law to himself, able totally to disregard (apart from a Patroclus or so) the interests of his fellows engaged with him in the joint venture. But nations, we note, still so conceive themselves, and cultivate along with this delusion, the accompanying vanity, ruthlessness, and irresponsibility. Why, with Alcibiades and others as familiar examples, Plato does not point up this side of the case against the Homeric ideal is for historians to answer. The actual influences from the *Iliad* favoring aristocratic self-centered regardlessness right through—wherever Homer has had a real part in educating ruling classes—are incontestable. That magnificent blond beast of prey has wreaked (and still does) not a little ruin throughout the course of the Hellenocentric tradition. Homer, long after his deposition in the *Republic*, has continued to shape the minds of the privileged in fashions very far from the collective human interest. Plato, in fact, was not nearly drastic enough. He was still far too much under Homer's spell. Similarly, those who have hitherto regarded the Bible as an influence misshaping man have been too lenient. They have not sharply enough directed attention to the reasons why it should be dethroned.

Such reasons in the case of the Bible appear near its beginnings: in the Lord God's grounds for sending Adam out of Eden (Gen. 3:22–24):

And the LORD God said, Behold, the man is become as one of us, to know good and evil; and now, lest he put forth his hand, and take also of the tree of life, and eat, and live for ever: therefore the LORD God sent him forth from the garden of Eden, to till the ground from whence he was taken.

So he drove out the man; and he placed at the east of the garden of Eden the Cherubim, and the flame of a sword which turned every way, to keep the way of the tree of life.

How strange a view of what it is to "become as one of us, to know good and evil" here appears! Next comes his arbitrary unexplained favoritism of Abel.

At a time when modern man's capacities for mass murder and for individual hand-gun killing are ever rising, it may be well to look closely and reflectively at what we learn from the Bible about the circumstances in which the first murder occurred. They are given with instructive fullness in Genesis (4:1–16):

And Adam knew Eve his wife; and she conceived, and bare Cain, and said, I have gotten a man from the LORD.

2   And she again bare his brother Abel. And Abel was a keeper of sheep, but Cain was a tiller of the ground.

3   And in process of time it came to pass, that Cain brought of the fruit of the ground an offering unto the LORD.

4   And Abel, he also brought of the firstlings of his flock and of the fat thereof. And the LORD had respect unto Abel and to his offering:

5   But unto Cain and to his offering he had not respect. And Cain was very wroth, and his countenance fell.

6   And the LORD said unto Cain, Why art thou wroth? and why is thy countenance fallen?

7   If thou doest well, shalt thou not be accepted? and if thou doest not well, sin lieth at the door. And unto thee shall be his desire, and thou shalt rule over him.

8   And Cain talked with Abel his brother: and it came to pass, when they were in the field, that Cain rose up against Abel his brother, and slew him.

9   And the LORD said unto Cain, Where is Abel thy brother? And he said, I know not: Am I my brother's keeper?

10   And he said, What hast thou done? the voice of thy brother's blood crieth unto me from the ground.

11   And now art thou cursed from the earth, which hath opened her mouth to receive thy brother's blood from thy hand;

12   When thou tillest the ground, it shall not henceforth yield unto thee her strength; a fugitive and a vagabond shalt thou be in the earth.

13   And Cain said unto the LORD, My punishment is greater than I can bear.

14   Behold, thou hast driven me out this day from the face of the earth; and from thy face shall I be hid; and I shall be a fugitive and a vagabond in the earth; and it shall come to pass, that every one that findeth me shall slay me.

15   And the LORD said unto him, Therefore whosoever slayeth Cain, vengeance shall be taken on him sevenfold. And the LORD set a mark upon Cain, lest any finding him should kill him.

16   And Cain went out from the presence of the LORD, and dwelt in the land of Nod, on the east of Eden.

The narrative order of verses 3–5 is subtly effective: Cain brings his offering and nothing is said about it. Then Abel brings his, which is well written-up. Follows at once its acceptance and Abel's. Only then are we told how, in contrast, both Cain and his offering are not found acceptable. Cain's wroth at this rebuff is not only great, but it is openly shown: "his countenance fell." This description is finely open to varied interpretation. He is angry; but is he also afraid? Does he know already why he and his offering are out of favor? Was his offering just what came handiest from his field, some old onions, say? Abel's was of his earliest lambs or kids and the choicest.

Several different readings can compete or combine here. A simple view is that Cain has failed to take this symbolic act—his offering—seriously enough. A more complex view: this shows that his respect for the Lord (along with his offering) was inadequate; he is slighting God, who accordingly slights him. Abel has been more respectful; some will rather say more prudent. (We can note here how layerlike such great narratives can be. We can go down and down from the surface reading.) We are likely, of course, and for centuries have been, to give to such ritual performances all manner of symbolic and spiritual significances that they perhaps never had for the first tellers of the tale. No matter; it is with the tale as understood in later periods that we are concerned here. But we, and readers at all times, will, with such a familiar story as this, inevitably well known already, read back into the opening moves what we know of the outcome. A large part of the power of a traditional story comes from the art with which its telling uses our prior knowledge. Since Cain is to be the first murderer, he must have been bad indeed from the start. And that cryptic verse 7—"sin lieth at the door. And unto thee shall be his desire, and thou shalt rule over him"—thus gains a dreadful inevitability: sin waiting upon Cain, ever eager and ready to do his bidding. This is the first personification of evil in the Bible, for the poor serpent seems to have been merely showing off his famous subtlety to Eve and his skill as the talking animal.

When the brothers talk together we may well wonder what Abel said to provoke what followed. Some variety of "I told you so!" maybe. Or did he mockingly repeat the Lord's questions? To give Cain the benefit of a doubt which he has, I suspect, frequently enjoyed, he might not have meant to kill Abel. This is the first human death, and Cain might have been as much surprised by it as Abel—a figure, I believe, that few have been much attached to. Cain's reply, too, to the Lord's question "Where is Abel thy brother?" may not be the evasion it has usually been supposed to be. How would Cain know where Abel, as opposed to his body, might be? And his following question, in place of condemning himself, may really be pointing at the Lord: You, so powerful and all-knowing, why did you not protect your Abel?

Special pleading, no doubt, all this. It is intended to bring out some natural antipathy towards the favored and sympathy for the guilty,[4] such as may be suspected to have often, in the

4. A puzzling expression of possible fellow-feeling for Cain can be found in Coleridge's "The Wanderings of Cain," the abandoned trial flight for *The Ancient Mariner*. Cain and his little son, Enos, find in the desert a Shape with printless feet that is like Abel. "And Cain said, 'Didst thou not find favour in the sight of the Lord thy God?' The Shape that was

The Scripture over You

oppressed schoolchild's wondering, accompanied the main lesson against murder. Plainly, in Cain, resentment felt, and perhaps duly, against the Lord has been discharged upon Abel. It will be noted that the concession made in verse 15 is hardly what it seems. That *sevenfold,* moreover, is as ruthless as it is obscure. All the problems of retributive justice are here in a nutshell.

Let us experimentally identify ourselves, as so many young readers do, with Cain, trying to occupy and adopt his viewpoint. As we do so, we may find that we know rather more about him than we might expect; for example, in comparing his position with that of the poet of Psalm 139 and with some of the positions among which Job shifts. In the first place, he is in his own eyes truly a victim. Whatever was amiss about his offering, he has— through its summarily unexplained rejection, putting the blame *all* on him as an appointed lord and patron of sin—been *made* a murderer, the first of all, the channel through which violence enters the world, a violence which *sevenfold* (v. 15) suggests is now to multiply rapidly. By Lamech's time (v. 24) the vengeance has, it seems, gone up to *seventy and sevenfold.* He, and indeed endless others, is to be punished for something which—as he sees it—is far from being wholly his fault. The curse from the earth, making his toil henceforth unfruitful and his condition fugitive and vagabond and putting him in fear for his life—though protected by that grim mark—makes his punishment much more an *example,* the subject of would-be deterrent action, than any evidence of his Punisher's wisdom. A grim paradigm of requitals is thus set before mankind in this most prominent place. No one can say that men have failed to follow it.

Three sentences back, with the word *example,* I switched from a reconstruction of Cain's view to the presentation of my own. I have used him enough, probably, to show why the dethronement of the Bible which is taking place is so much overdue, and why much contemporary opinion blaming current growth in violence

---

like Abel answered, 'The Lord is God of the living only, the dead have another God.' Then the child Enos lifted up his eyes and prayed; but Cain rejoiced secretly in his heart."

on the lapse of Heaven-Hell sanctions has been mistaken. It is
the use of those sanctions through so long a period, the warping
of men's minds by attempting to induce obedience through
torments and requitals, that has put us where we are. We shall
not help ourselves by any returns to the wrong courses that the
effective parts of the Bible as a whole have inculcated. (Merciless
their heels have been!) We will be wiser to remember, against
whatever distractions, what it is in man on which his worth
depends and what in his search for good he is truly seeking.

To revert, however, to the over-all influence exerted by the
Bible, "the Scripture over us," presenting with unparalleled
authority, through the most malleable, the least protected years
of our growth, its image of Authority itself. Let us go back to
Genesis 3:22: "Behold the man is become as one of us, to know
good and evil." "As one of us"? What must happen for any
tradition—Judean, Edomitic, Hellenic, Christian—if we represent
the ideal source of justice, our exemplar of order, our model of
integrity, in terms of such frailty and (from this Lord God's point
of view) such sinfulness as Eve's and Adam's? It is an enthrone-
ment of irresponsibility, of lack of self-control, of self-centered
disregard of its victims at the very point—our Idea of the Good—
from which all our moral effort should depend. What is done in
Genesis is perhaps not really worse than the goings-on of the
Olympians, or than the antics with those lots presided over by
that "sort of prophet," spokesman for Lachesis, daughter of
Necessity, in Plato's myth of Er, or than the moral nihilism of
Shaddai's shoutings. But it has a peculiar evil in attributing all
our woes to a failure to obey *blindly* a command from a Ruler
who is depicted as manifestly arbitrary, irresponsible, incompetent, and unjust. The effect is that human rulers, judges, school-
masters, persons in authority everywhere who may have their
share of these same characteristics gain a shelter from this image
of the divine. People come to expect presidents and such to
behave like God.

To continue with the reasons why the models of human and
divine behavior pressed upon us by the Bible for so long have

been so far from salutary. The vacillations and repentances of the affair of the flood (Gen. 6:5–8, 8:20–21) have often been noted; less so the unmodel conduct of the chosen man Abram in Egypt (Gen. 12:11–20), conduct repeated with Abimalech (Gen. 20). Now comes God's tempting of the renamed Abraham to offer Isaac "Thine only son whom thou lovest . . . for a burnt offering" (Gen. 22). This was to be a test of how much Abraham "feared God," and we may again remind ourselves that the Old Testament has no other name for religion than "the fear of God." We come now to the performances of the chief culture hero, Jacob, renamed Israel at the Jabok ford. His dealings with Esau hardly need recounting: the buying of the birthright exploiting his brother's need (Gen. 25:29–34); the elaborate lying theft of the blind Isaac's blessing (Gen. 27, especially 16–24). Isaac's suspicions are noteworthy: he had had reason to know Jacob.

What is notable about these doings is that they are immediately rewarded by his ladder dream at Bethel, by God's personal promise of "the land whereon thou liest" and of descendants "as the dust of the earth" (Abram was only promised them "as the stars"). What is equally interesting is the carefully provisional character of the vow this frightened but wary man commits himself to. Though in the night he has said: "How dreadful is this place! This is none other than the house of God, and this is the gate of heaven" (Gen. 28:17), in the morning it is: "If God will be with me . . . then shall the Lord be my God . . . and of all that thou shalt give me I will surely give the tenth unto thee" (28:20–22).

After fourteen years with Laban and further characteristically clever doings by which he has become possessed of most of Laban's wealth—with the full approval of the God of his vow at Bethel—Jacob, with his two wives, his children, his people, and all that he has, departs secretly to return home. Rachel, his loved wife, steals, unknown to Jacob, her father's teraphim (household gods, on which Laban's prosperity might depend). Laban catches up with Jacob, who says: "With whomsoever thou findest thy gods, let him not live" (31:32). Laban searches

Rachel's tent, but "Rachel had taken the images and put them in the camel's furniture, and sat upon them. And Laban searched all the tent, but found them not" (31:34). How important those teraphim must have been to Laban! And what father-daughter relationships this scene suggests! Rachel pleads her menses as reason for not rising, so the teraphim are not found. It looks as if Rachel had learned some useful things from her husband. Laban and Jacob then make a pact of nonaggression and build a pile of stones as witness to it. Jacob swears "By the fear of his father Isaac." Isaac, knowing (we assume) of Abraham's obedient readiness to make a burned sacrifice of him, had grounds for fearing. This comment seems but modern levity, until we consider how many generations of our forebears were brought up ("lessoned" under the rod) to take that story in and weigh it as God's Holy Word, and in what regard mere unquestioning obedience, especially for the impressionable child, used to be held.

Then follows one of the most potent and mysterious passages in the Old Testament, Jacob's wrestle with whatever met him at Peniel. From this he gained his new name, Israel, for "as a prince hast thou power with God and with men and hast prevailed" (32:28). We may well feel that Jacob here is certainly not being *under*praised. Enormous though the discussion of this reported occurrence has been, the question whether the only reporter must have been Jacob himself, with his limp to prove his tale, has been, through most of it, obscured by the premise that all this is God's word recorded somehow in the first book of Moses. But the extent and depth of the influence of Genesis 32:24-31 on history makes no question that can be raised about the passage any laughing matter.

From these queer problems it is an astonishing relief to step into Chapter 33, describing Jacob's meeting with Esau. Amid the trembling and bowing multitudes of Jacob's following, with Jacob coming forward, at last, "bowing himself to the ground seven times until he came near to his brother," Esau, the one decent, openhearted character we have yet met, "ran to meet him, and embraced him, and fell on his neck and kissed him"

(33:4). But, alas, false notes are soon to be heard in Jacob's speech, following Esau's refusal of all those excessive and so carefully calculated presents (33:9–10, my italics):

And Esau said: I have enough, my brother; keep that thou hast unto thyself.

And Jacob said, Nay, I pray thee, if now I have found grace in thy sight, then receive my present at my hand: for *therefore* I have seen thy face, *as though I had seen the face of God,* and thou wast pleased with me.

In *therefore,* the overly shrewd reminder: "Come now, we both know what has done it." And the would-be compensating balm in the unctuous hyperbole that follows. It fits well with his Bethel dream and vow and with what he has told Rachel and Leah of this "in the field beside his flock" (31:13).

From very early days, with the first gathering of the stories which came together to be the canon, the tradition was that Genesis was the first book of Moses. Questions about the stories —about who told them first, who put them together, and so on— which naturally occur to a modern reader, never arose. The stories were just part of the inspired Holy Scriptures and were to be received as such. The degree of incuriosity, the numbing of reflective inquiry that such an assumption imposes is something that a reader today may find hard to conceive. The questions animating my selection of the items listed could hardly have been asked; they would have been too perverse and iniquitous. But should we say unlikely "to occur" or "to be formulated"? Plenty of questions can occur in a child's mind before it has learned, and grimly, that some of these are acceptable, some not. Writing now, in a decade in which fashion has ruled that for the time being little should be mentioned but the unmentionable, I need hardly labor such a point. We have to remind ourselves that, not long ago, fashion as firmly commanded absolute respect for Holy Writ.

My list of items of questionable motivation and conduct (with references supplied because all this will be far less well known than would have been the case only a few decades back) can be continued by any selective eye right through the Bible. My sample from the earliest stories is enough, I think, to show its slant. The Old Testament is a vast, accretive, collective work vivified above all by a need to present and exalt Israel as a people beyond all others, being chosen of old by God to be his people. And I have been picking out dubious things in the conduct of its founding fathers—things questionable, for the most part, rather to childish, immature, untutored minds, than to adults, things to be kept under, for covert, if any, reflection and not to be voiced or discussed in the pulpit. That such things are there in abundance and yet have been so little remarked is indeed one of the inexhaustible mysteries about the Bible. Its texts have been much tinkered with; and yet so much that any modern propagandist would censor remains.

The modern selective eye, if it continued its list, would be able to enter an extraordinary number and variety of points against this people, points which seem to go directly against any propaganda purpose—as if it were their faults and weaknesses rather than their strengths which had led to their being chosen. "How odd/Of God/To choose/The Jews!" a list maker will find himself muttering. Some of this unfortunate behavior has long been notorious: for instance, their murmurings in the Sinai deserts. All readers' hearts have always ached for Moses. And yet how deeply Exodus influences Dante's world picture. Some has been less noticed: after the conquests in Canaan, for example, the experiment in genocide tried out by "all the children of Israel" on "the children of Benjamin" (Judg. 19–21). And for other arresting reading: about what happened to a people living in Laish, "quiet and secure" at the hands of "the children of Dan," and of the role of a graven image and a molten image and teraphim in all this, try chapters 17 and 18 of Judges. We can see here why (though from very much an opposing angle) Coleridge framed the title of his lay sermon, as Bate finely puts it, with "brave innocence": *The Stateman's Manual: or the Bible*

The Scripture over You

the Best Guide to Political Skill and Foresight. It is indeed, of all books, that from which the saddest, gravest lessons may be learned—among them, no doubt, some that are most salutary. But let us be concerned here rather with the disturbing fact that, through the ages, so many readers from their various viewpoints have learned from it—*unconsciously as much as consciously*—so many extraordinarily corruptive lessons. Among these lessons unconsciously (or semiconsciously) learned there are some that may be of truly frightening present moment.

Anti-Semitism, that dread socio-psychic disease, is not a matter that, with memories of Hitler still living and with current tensions as they are, should be taken less seriously than cancer. Its etiology is without doubt very complex, needing study from many points of view so related that better understanding of any one of the converging factors may be a help. Among these, it seems surprising that influences from the Bible have not been more fully and more penetratingly considered. There are, it is true, preventive obstacles. Here, once again, we are in a self-reflexive situation. A study of how the Jews appear, are presented, in the Bible is liable to be regarded as itself anti-Semitic or, on the contrary, as propagandistic. Moreover, useful reflections are likely to be lost in irrelevant discussions of the composition of the Bible itself, arguments about why various sources in it may have represented things as they did, why redactors, often at indeterminable dates, changed the accounts—often adding verses which would have much puzzled the sources—and so on. Those readers who look through chapters 18–21 of Judges will note the refrain: "In those days there was no king in Israel: every man did that which was right in his own eyes." The mixed materials in those chapters, put together for various purposes at various dates, are there because their final editor (a monarchist) thought such dreadful stories would convey a useful moral. But what matters here is how the compilation has been read, not how it was put together. Such details are for scholars and have nothing to do with any effects passages may produce on impressionable minds (unbeknownst to them or not).

Beyond

These and other distractions may well explain insufficient attention to this possible root of anti-Semitism. Setting them aside, as far as we may, let us consider the over-all situation. Here we have the most authoritative of all books establishing the unique and supreme status of Israel. It does so both in passage after passage of the Old Testament and through its general progression; and, in the New Testament, through the hero being a Jew, bearer and fulfilment of Israel's prophecy and hope. And for the readers on whom the Bible has been binding there is to be no blinking at any of this, no eyebrow-lifting, no lip-pursing. It is so. All other peoples everywhere and through all time are thus inalienably and immeasurably indebted to Israel, who prepared for and produced their Savior. And this claim (far more than a claim, a *ruling*) has had to be simply accepted. That is what its long-term students through nearly two millennia took as necessary. (Look up *millennium* in the Dictionary, and you will recover, if you need it, something of the taste of the positions imposed on the readers we should be thinking of; there are often divines, and should be, among lexicographers.) Is it to be wondered at if the attitudes of the culture such readers shaped happens to be—shall we say—ambivalent? It would be more than human not to feel at times the pressures of such obligations irksome. And have we not known, since the opening of Book IX of the *Republic* (571 on, a thumbnail sketch of how Hitler came about), that sternly-enough-suppressed impulses can take their revenges? Is it not likely that suppressed attitudes of Biblical origin can make situations that are dangerous already still more hazardous? This people is favored by the Lord. Favorites, as we know (witness Abel), have often to suffer from resentments really felt against the Favorer.

Epilogue

The Holy Word

Look we both at and through
Bronze and lacquer and stone.

In the Prologue there was insistence that actual situations are tokens only and that "the SITUATION they exemplify and represent (their type) . . . is the guide . . . as to what is being said and what it is we may have to do." A combining of that type-token opposition with the $\frac{T}{V}$ relationship (where V is what we look *at* and that *through* which we would apprehend T) can serve as a useful terminal reminder. Without pretense at answering them it may present its questions with what may be an invigorating freshness. At first, the attempt to use *together* both these mnemonic devices may seem to invite confusion. Each would have us remember what we are doing—but in differing respects; $\frac{T}{V}$ recalls that in all selecting, ascribing, imaging, valuing, endeavoring, we have to do with Bradley's curtain, Tenors being behind or before it. Type-token recalls that in all our activities we have to do with instances, occurrents—not directly with what

179

is instanced, with what occurs. (The Prologue tried to say what it could about the various ways of conceiving this relationship.) Jointly, they would have us accept a somewhat different role as participants from that which we ordinarily assume—whether it is a humbler or a more exalted role (or both) remains to be seen. Do we not commonly suppose ourselves to be fully (or at least sufficiently) conversant with what we are dealing with—dressing the Tenors present to us in vestments as we please? (Cf. Dante's "garb of figure and colour.") Do we not equally suppose that as types we manifest ourselves in our appearances?

A question, this, which, if overpressed, can be distressing. The sharpest applications (instances) come when we consider our own instabilities, our own yearly, daily, hourly, momently occurrences, and ask what is the occurrent, the type which thus recurs. The incessant variations of our token-streams are represented by plenty of ways of talking about our true selves, about being beside ourselves or only too much ourselves, as with Housman's young hero:

> And miles around they'll say that I
> Am quite myself again.

And so on. In taking this situation as seriously as it would certainly seem to deserve, an experimental $\frac{T}{V}$ type-token conjunction may be a help.

A discomfort we should feel with the type-token formulation (as with those others compared in the Prologue) comes from our so readily supposing that tokens (in contrast to types) are beings of low status: inherently of inferior worth and dignity. The supposition should not survive the reflection that types are wholly dependent on and derivative from their tokens. We know nothing of them but as means by which we attempt to account for the order among tokens. It is with tokens only that we deal, and only as tokens ourselves can we deal with them.[1] Our recognition of

1. Together with a feeling that tokens are inferior to types goes a tendency to suppose that types must be eternal (or at least unchanging), while

Epilogue: The Holy Word

all this has a curious ambivalence in outcome. We become representatives, and that seems a modest role. But representatives of what? A question some aspects of which can well satisfy anyone's ambitions. As I write this, I am aware of how entirely this vehicle may be misread.

"To be as gods knowing good and evil." Have many, freely pondering the Fall, been without their deep reverberant sympathies with Lucifer's and Eve's decisions, together with a shrinking from the responsibility entailed? It was urged above that we can no more know good without knowing evil than we can know here without there or now without then.

To be thus involved, made responsible, required to choose, is another thing from merely being able to suffer as well as to enjoy. Job's words at the end of the folk-tale prelude—"What? Shall we receive good at the hand of God, and shall we not receive evil?" (2:10)—point only to the latter, though that other Job of the poem again and again contrasts his own moral being (Chapter 31) with the clear lack of any such thing in Shaddai. This engagement in the conduct of the Universe comes from our status as tokens of the type Man, and carries the capacity to do evil as well as good and also, as part of that, the ability—only too often impaired—to see *which* of them we are doing.

If we accept such a position (weighing it against others, a weighing itself a case of seeing *which* we are doing), many attitudes for living are favored which any appeal to omnipotence, say, or any undue concern for our own personal fate, will shut out. We come near to what is described in the passage from William James adduced in the Prologue as exemplifying the Conceptualist temper.

---

tokens are variable and fleeting. But, in these uses, we need give types no more persistence than is required by the order we are describing with their aid. Man, for example, is the most variable of creatures. We need not pretend that there is more constancy in his type than we find it convenient to allow. He has developed and, we trust, will go on developing— to become more what we think we ought to be. For further discussion of this position I can now refer to the chapters on "Logical Machinery" in my *Interpretation in Teaching*.

Beyond

Its opening sentences invite another conjuncture: that with the Bradley/Hegel/Attar-Fitzgerald/Psalm 139 speculations (Chapter 5) as to what is *behind* us when we confront what is before us. (It is interesting to recall what doughty philosophical opponents William James and Bradley were.) In place of Hegel, Bradley might well have quoted, for a fuller account, Coleridge —from his *Essay XI On the Principles of Method* in *The Friend* (Vol. 1, p. 509):

Man sallies forth into nature—in nature, as in the shadows and reflections of a clear river, to discover the originals of the forms presented to him in his own intellect. Over these shadows, as if they were the substantial powers and presiding spirits of the stream, Narcissus-like, he hangs delighted: till finding nowhere a representative of that free agency which yet is a *fact* of immediate consciousness sanctioned and made fearfully significant by his prophetic *conscience,* he learns at last that what he *seeks* he has *left behind,* and but lengthens the distance as he prolongs the search. Under the tutorage of scientific ANALYSIS, haply first given to him by express revelation (e coelo descendit, Γνῶθι σεαυτον) * he separates the *relations* that are wholly the creatures of his own abstracting and comparing intellect, and at once discovers and recoils from the discovery, that the *reality,* the *objective* truth, of the objects he has been adoring, derives its whole and sole evidence from an obscure sensation, which he is alike unable to resist or to comprehend, which compels him to contemplate as without and independent of himself what yet he could not contemplate at all, were it not a modification of his own being.

* "From heaven it descends, *Know thyself*" (Juvenal's *Satires* XI, 27).

There is much that may perplex here. It will prevent undue certainties to append a balancing passage from a note written by S. T. C. on a flyleaf. It may serve me, through the switchings it suggests among our means of knowing, as a summing up of these so many pages. (See Kathleen Coburn, *Enquiring Spirit,* item 318.)

Epilogue: The Holy Word

318. AN ALLEGORY

A beautiful Allegory of Persian Wisdom—its analogy to Prometheus—
to Satan or Lucifer, etc.

Anahid, the Egyptian Nëith, the Greek Athene = Logos, Verstand.†
Harut and Murat, who obtained permission to descend from Heaven
and become incarnate as Men, in order to try the sensual nature, and
the possibility of its subordination to the Spiritual—bringing with
them the Holy Word (Idea, Λόγος πρωτογένης) by which they de-
scended and were enabled to re-ascend. But they became sensually
enamoured of Anahid, who gave them hopes of yielding herself to
their embraces, on condition of their communicating the Holy Word.
Instead of trying they [were] *tempted,* and they gave the Word to
Anahid—which instantly was lost to them, forgotten—and in the same
instant, Anahid soared to the Morning Star (Phosphor) and with her
harp strung with sunbeams, plays to the Spheres, the Goddess of Love
and Order. H[arut] and M[urat] = Reason and Will.

† Elsewhere, he is, on the whole, rather hard on the Understanding, assigning to it as proper function "generalizing the notices received from the
senses," a power concerned with "the cold mechanism of a worthless
because compulsory assent"; a power moreover whose deathly trespassing
on the functions of Reason and Will was the continuing curse of his (and
our) age. But here, and in some other places, a larger and wilder surmise
awakens in him.

Our dealings with the "Knowers of knowledge": Reason, Will, and Understanding are too near us not to be out of sight. Here is another version
of the passage from "The Famous Debates in the Forest" (not at all Dante's
selva oscura) quoted in the Prologue, footnote 3:

Yadnyawalkya said, "You cannot see the seer of seeing, or hear the hearer
of hearing, or think the thinker of thought, or know the knower. It is your
own self that lives in the hearts of all. All else is vanity."

How bold the play of the opening and closing equations here!
That Coleridge could do this with Understanding and Reason
and Will—how liberating! Understanding—through H's and M's
fault—becomes Lucifer-Phosphor, the Morning Star which shall,
in due course, become Hesper, the Evening Star. (What that
discovery must have meant to those first systematizing watchers
of the skies!) How deep a transformation comes about through
the imparting of the Holy Word we may realize through the

Beyond

contrast between Dante's Dis and this Anahid, now harping Goddess of Love and Order, two august powers indeed. Love as Agape, here. And Order as the most ultimate and infinitely explorable idea we have. Both terms liable, nonetheless, to every sort of mistaking and confusion—from that in which Adah and Lucifer indulge in Byron's *Cain: a Mystery:*

> *Adah:* I have heard it said,
> The seraphs *love most*—cherubim *know most*—
> And this should be a cherub—since he loves not.
> *Lucifer:* And if the higher knowledge quenches love,
> What must *he be* you cannot love when known?
> Since the all-knowing cherubim love least,
> The seraphs' love can be but ignorance:

on up to poor H's and M's (Reason's and Will's) undoing.

For Byron's characters here, 'Love' is Eros not Agape, and the 'Knowledge' thus opposed seems no more than that of Anahid unpossessed as yet of any Holy Word. The great speech in which Lucifer initiates Cain should be compared. As opposed to what the seraphs sing and say,

> on pain
> Of being that which I am—and thou art—
> Of spirits and of men,

Lucifer and Cain are

> Souls who dare use their immortality—
> Souls who dare look the Omnipotent tyrant in
> His everlasting face, and tell him that
> His evil is not good! If he has made
> As he saith—which I know not, nor believe—
> But, if he made us—he cannot unmake:
> We are immortal! nay, he'd *have* us so,
> That he may torture:—let him! He is great—
> But, in his greatness, is no happier than
> We in our conflict: Goodness would not make
> Evil; and what else hath he made? But let him
> Sit on his vast and solitary throne,

Epilogue: The Holy Word

Creating worlds, to make eternity
Less burthensome to his immense existence
And unparticipated solitude;
Let him crowd orb on orb: he is alone.
Indefinite, indissoluble tyrant,
Could he but crush himself, 'twere the best boon
He ever granted.

A voice of hate, indeed, which we will do well to compare, and at some length, with the speech in which Shelley's Prometheus overcomes and, through Demogorgon, dethrones Jupiter (*Prometheus Unbound* I, 53–58):

Disdain! Ah no! I pity thee. What ruin
Will hunt thee undefended through wide Heaven!
How will thy soul, cloven to its depth with terror,
Gape like a hell within! I speak in grief,
Not exultation, for I hate no more,
As then ere misery made me wise.

These lines are Shelley's version of "the Holy Word" that so transformed Anahid.

Three passages in *Prometheus Unbound*, if we linger with them till they reflect one another, will best summarize and confirm what I have hoped will be the over-all import of my chapters. These three are the colloquy between Asia and Demogorgon (II, 4, 1–30), the transfiguration of Asia which follows (II, 5, 6–47), and the account given by Prometheus in the renovated world of the role of Poetry and the Arts (III, 3, 6–63).

The strange figure of Demogorgon at the very heart of the play has naturally been the occasion of much discussion. We may, however, suppose that Shelley was well advised to leave him, whose name, on his own lips, is Eternity—together with his action in the overthrow of Jupiter, and his relation to

The snake-like Doom coiled underneath his throne—

as indefinite as they are. He is a Presence of immense authority, and his interrogation by Asia well represents our own obstinate

Beyond

questionings of whatever sources we can find. When therefore under her somewhat indocile pressure he replies, we will do well to take his words to heart:

> *Demogorgon:* If the abysm
> Could vomit forth its secrets. . . . But a voice
> Is wanting, the deep truth is imageless.

This is extraordinarily expressive, coming as near as may be to serving as an image of the imageless.

The opening of the scene should fully prepare us for this outcome:

> *Panthea:* What veilèd form sits on that ebon throne?
> *Asia:* The veil has fallen.
> *Panthea:* I see a mighty darkness
> Filling the seat of power, and rays of gloom
> Dart round, as light from the meridian sun.

In reading this we should, I think, let Panthea's words represent what the two sisters jointly see. There is no hint anywhere in the play that she is to be regarded as especially purblind, however much she may be second to her great sister.[2]

As we read on to the end of the scene we find Panthea's description of Demogorgon's ascent in the dark chariot of his hour fully accepted by Asia:

2. I cannot therefore agree with Mr. Neville Rogers when he writes: "Asia's eyes can see more—'The veil has fallen,' she cries. This means, in terms of the Veil-symbol characteristically grafted on to the Cave symbol, that she can perceive light bursting into the cave—the radiance, due to the lifting of the Veil by Prometheus's love, is imperceptible to Panthea." *Shelley at Work* (London: Oxford, 1967), p. 156. Mr. Rogers thinks that Asia in Demogorgon's cave is being prepared for her coming union with Prometheus. But see Prometheus' words in Act I, lines 809–11:

> Asia! who, when my being overflowed,
> Wert like a golden chalice to bright wine
> Which else had sunk into the thirsty dust.

See also Panthea's last speech in Act I. The ether of Asia's transforming presence has long been mingled with that of Prometheus. She is, indeed, his *Shakti*.

Epilogue: The Holy Word

watch its path among the stars
Blackening the night!
Asia: Thus am I answered: strange!

Moreover, the spirit of that hour itself declares:

the darkness which ascends with me
Shall wrap in lasting night heaven's Kingless throne.

There is nothing whatever in all this about light or radiance visible to Asia alone.

Surely this very darkness that the play is here presenting with some insistence is no strange thing in this connection—though we must take care, no doubt, not to confuse it with other darknesses, any more than we should confuse Demogorgon with other objects of meditation in the mystical tradition.

Demogorgon, like Asia herself, and even Jupiter, is a "shadow," an "image": a representation partial and selective of that about which she has been questioning him. If, with Paul Tillich,[3] we suppose that "an unmythical treatment" of the unconditioned transcendent, "a language without symbols," is in some way possible, this negativism of Demogorgon can be taken as a token of that very treatment. Jupiter is overthrown not only because absolute power has utterly corrupted him—

To know nor faith, nor love, nor law; to be
Omnipotent but friendless is to reign

—as Asia pronounces (II, 4, 47); and not only because his continuance in office would destroy "the soul of man" which

Yet burns to heaven with fierce reproach, and doubt
And lamentation, and reluctant prayer;

Jupiter has to go because he is a characterization, and a particularly vicious and poisoning characterization, of that which can in no way be characterized. *Neti, neti;* but, above all, *not* Jupiter. "Whereof one cannot speak, thereof one must be silent." [4]

3. See, for example, "The Religious Symbol" in *Daedalus,* Journal of the American Academy of Arts and Sciences, Summer 1958, p. 20.
4. Wittgenstein, *Tractatus Logico-Philosophicus.* Final proposition.

Beyond

Shelley knows what he is doing too well to set any substitute on Jupiter's throne. Rejection of all occupants of that throne is a prime recurrent element of his poetry. Not Demogorgon, not even Prometheus, can safely be accorded any such power. A few sentences from Tillich's essay mentioned above make an interesting commentary upon Shelley's celebrated atheism (pp.14–15):

> The divine beings and the Supreme Being, God, are representations of that which is ultimately referred to in the religious act. They are representations, for the unconditioned transcendent surpasses every possible conception of a being, including even the conception of a Supreme Being. In so far as any such being is assumed as existent it is again annihilated in the religious act. In this annihilation, in this atheism immanent in the religious act, the profoundest aspect of the religious act is manifest.

Shelley's youthful pamphlet, *The Necessity of Atheism,* contained no more than a provocative agnosticism. His notorious "There is no God" (*Queen Mab,* VII, 13) carried the note: "This negation must be understood solely to affect a creative Deity. The hypothesis of a pervading Spirit coeternal with the universe remains unshaken." No doubt, as he remarked to Trelawney, he used the word *atheist* as "painted devil to frighten the foolish, a threat to intimidate the wise and good." (We have, I suppose, to imagine ironical derision marks around ¡wise¡ and ¡good¡ here.) "I used it," he goes on, "to express my abhorrence of superstition; I took up the word as a knight took up a gauntlet in defiance of injustice." Some of this may be Trelawney. But when, in 1816, in the album at the Montanvert and again in the album at the Hotel de Londres at Chamouni (and maybe elsewhere) Shelley described himself, in Greek lettering, as "democrat, great lover of mankind, and atheist," part of the explanation of a gesture that was to do him great harm may have been the perception soon to be embodied in Demogorgon.

In *Prometheus Unbound,* Demogorgon further embodies the offspring of Jupiter's union with Thetis: a union vauntingly described by Jupiter in lines which have a fascinating obverse relation to those with which—at that very moment—the Voice in the Air (originally Prometheus) is celebrating Asia's transfiguration (compare III, 1, 33–47 with II, 5, 47–71). The Numidian seps put by Jupiter into Thetis' mouth is a stroke of Shelley's satire which will be missed if we do not look the reference up in Lucan (*Pharsalia* IX, 763–88):

But a more sad death than that was before their eyes; and upon the thigh of the wretched Sabellius there stood a little Seps, which, hanging with its barbed tooth, he both tore off with his hand, and pinned with his javelin to the sand; a little serpent only, but than which not one is so sure a source of a bloody death. For the skin nearest the wound, torn off, disappears, and discloses the pallid bones. And now with open surface, without a body left, the wound is bare; the limbs swim in corrupt matter; the calves fall off; without any covering are the hams; of the thighs, too, every muscle is dissolved, and the groin distils black matter. The membrane that binds the stomach snaps asunder, and the bowels flow away; nor does just so much of the entire body as may be expected flow upon the earth, but the raging venom melts the limbs; soon does the poison convert all the ligaments of the nerves, and the textures of the sides, and the hollow breast, and what is concealed in the vital lungs, everything that composes man, into a diminutive corrupt mass. By a foul death does nature lie exposed; the shoulders and strong arms melt; the neck and head flow away.

Not more quickly does the snow fall away, dissolved by the warm south wind, nor is wax influenced by the sun. Trifling things I mention, how that the body flowed away scorched up by corruption; this flame can do as well. But what pyre has ever dissolved the bones? These, too, disappear, and, following the crumbling marrow, suffer no vestiges of their rapid destruction to remain.

Choice reading for Olympians. This seps, ancestor to our word *septic,* is the very thing for Jupiter to identify himself with at such a juncture. This archpoisoner, who has been encouraging "heaven's winged hound" with a kiss when sending him out to tear up Prometheus's heart, hails Thetis as "bright image of eternity." Since it is Jupiter who is speaking, there is no reason to think she is that. (Plato's Demiurge in *Timaeus* (37D) creates

Beyond

Time to be "a moving likeness of Eternity" but no such parallels are in place here.)

On Demogorgon's arrival Jupiter is plainly taken aback by what moves towards him:

> Awful shape, what art thou? Speak!

The expected son and ally against the soul of man was not to be like this. Demogorgon replies:

> Eternity. Demand no direr name.

Neither this, nor the sonship to Jupiter which he acknowledges, nor his self-imposed exile with his father—

> we must dwell together
> Henceforth in darkness

—makes Demogorgon any the less baffling. But to be baffling, in fact, is his duty and business in the play. He and Jupiter fall together. It is true that Demogorgon makes a curtain appearance at the end of Act 4, lending his voice and authority to high prophecy, but as participant in the action he leaves with Jupiter, a cloud of impenetrable darkness to the end.

He has, however, in his colloquy with Asia added an affirmation to his denial. "It would avail nothing," he says (I, 4, 119),

> to bid speak
> Fate, Time, Occasion, Chance, and Change.

Among these, it may be noted, can be found both the Greek and the eighteenth-century versions of Necessity—the label usually attached to Demogorgon: the Greek view making Necessity "the indeterminate, the inconstant, the anomalous," to quote Grote on the *Timaeus;* and the eighteenth century using the opposite notion of a fixed causal chain. Such powers are not responsible here, great though they are. Demogorgon affirms:

> To these
> All things are subject but eternal Love.

Epilogue: The Holy Word

This echoes what Prometheus has declared:

> Most vain all hope but love;

And Asia now assents, adding a comment of the deepest significance:

> of such truths
> Each to itself must be the oracle.

Demogorgon's realm, it may be noted, is (II, 3, 4):

> Whence the oracular vapour is hurled up.

Asia is showing in this her characteristic and, I think, distinctly feminine independence. She is, throughout, quite undaunted by the "terrible shadow" confronting her. But then she herself, though she seems not in the least to know it, is the personification, the very incarnation of the one thing not subject to Fate, Time, Occasion, Chance, or Change: eternal Love.

She does not know it, and she is not in the least aware, in this scene, of what has really brought about Prometheus's triumph and the arrival of the defeated Jupiter's hour of doom. That triumph occurs as early as the lines I have already quoted from Act I.

So early comes the turning point of this play. A reader who—as W. B. Yeats hoped his fellow students would—rereads *Prometheus Unbound* "as a sacred book" would remember how Jupiter in his extremity cries (III, 1, 65–6):

> Oh,
> That thou wouldst make mine enemy my judge,
> . . . he would not doom me thus.

But of this redeeming, renovating change—the product of three thousand years of pain—Asia has not yet heard. At least, she has not yet taken it in. Whereas Jupiter, desperately pleading, can describe Prometheus as "Gentle, and just, and dreadless" (III, 1, 67), Asia can cry of Jupiter (II, 4, 30):

Beyond

Utter his name: a world pining in pain
Asks but his name: curses shall drag him down.

She is three thousand years out of date. Those were Prometheus' feelings when he uttered the great and splendid curse at the time of his enchainment.

Asia's violent demands (II, 4, 29) upon Demogorgon, who displays a patience commensurate with his presumable foreknowledge, are both an echo of Prometheus as she had known him at their separation and the prelude to a lecture on the history of civilization with which she puts her pressure on Demogorgon. It succeeds, but she does not—even now—know why. When Demogorgon ascends on his way to dethrone Jupiter, Asia is still wondering:

Thus I am answered: strange!

What has not been revealed to her is soon revealed through her (II, 5, 8). Panthea is the first to observe what is occurring: Asia is being transfigured.

Panthea: How thou art changed! I dare not look on thee;
I feel but see thee not. I scarce endure
The radiance of thy beauty.

Then follows a description of Botticelli's "The Birth of Venus" which was in the Uffizi Gallery, Florence, while Shelley, who took a keen interest in Italian paintings, was there in the fall of 1819.[5]

5. As E. H. Gombrich has now shown, in *Symbolic Images* (London: Phaidon, 1972), Botticelli, influenced by Neoplatonic ideas through Marsilio Ficino, "succeeded in opening up to secular art spheres which had hitherto been the preserve of religious worship." His Venus is as remote as may be from the sensual and stands not for Venery, but for Humanitas: for "love and charity, dignity and magnanimity, liberty and magnificence, comeliness and modesty, charm and splendor." Fittingly, then, Panthea ends her account with

nor is it I alone . . .
But the whole world which seeks thy sympathy,
Hearest thou not sounds i' the air which speak the love
Of all articulate beings? Feelest thou not
The inanimate winds enamoured of thee? List!

Epilogue: The Holy Word

Some good change [*Panthea* conceives]
Is working in the elements, which suffer
Thy presence thus unveiled.

Now comes the Voice in the Air (originally, it seems, that of Prometheus) which sings the passage of transfigured Asia, "Life of Life," to the release of Prometheus; and Asia's reply—closing with the reverted account [6] of human life from old age to pre-birth

Through Death and Birth to a diviner day.

The "paradise of wildernesses" thus traversed leads to another paradise (II, 5, 108):

Peopled by shapes too bright to see.

As whatever Demogorgon symbolizes is formless through extremity of darkness, so the vision of the Renovated World tends to become invisible, unimaginable, through radiance. Shelley has the wisdom and restraint not to attempt any but indirect descriptions. He knew that even a Dante must despair of words. As Beatrice tells Dante (*Par.* XXX, 76–81):

The river, the topazes that enter and come forth, the smiling grasses, are shadowy foretastes of their reality. Not that these things are themselves imperfect; but on thy side is the defect, in that thy vision cannot yet rise so high.

—so Shelley has to translate, has to find a language of dream, of indirect representation, for the reality he would lead us into.

The action of *Prometheus Unbound* is singular, I believe, in being essentially completed at the fifty-third line of the play. The remainder is outcome and reverberation from Prometheus's moral triumph there recorded. This, of course, entailed a prodigious task of invention and design upon the author, but did not

---

6. This reversal may be an echo of Plato, *Politicus* 270–73: the golden age returns when the pilot of the universe takes the helm again and then the direction of events is again reversed.

Beyond

find him short of resources. The hardest part of his task, perhaps, was to find something for Prometheus himself and his circle to do after his triumph.

His greeting to Asia when he is unbound can tell us much and prepare us to read what follows with a more discerning eye:

> Asia, thou light of life,
> Shadow of beauty unbeheld.[7]

We should be remembering as we read that it is the transfigured Asia he is saluting: the "Child of Light," the "Lamp of Earth" the Presence the Voice in the Air has been describing. It is this which is still "Shadow of beauty unbeheld." Even beyond and beyond beyond . . . It is this, I suggest, that is the most characteristic note of Shelley's mysticism: all lights are but tokens, veils, shadows, "vanishing apparitions which haunt the interlunations of life," as he says in *Defence of Poetry,* where poets, too, and their words are "hierophants of an *unapprehended* inspiration," "words which express *what they understand not*" (my italics). Even Asia here is such a word and so, too, is the Cave on which Prometheus now lavishes description, a dull reading of which will easily find as strained and artificial as Dante's topazes. But

> a fountain
> Leaps in the midst with an awakening sound.

This Cave—with the account the Earth gives later of how to reach it:

7. Again I cannot agree with Mr. Rogers that "Shadow has been displaced by *light*. No longer is Asia 'unbeheld' since she has been unveiled" (*Shelley at Work,* p. 130). This, it seems to me, would be a sad confusion of the visible and the indivisible of a kind which Shelley's knowledge of Plato would make improbable:

". . . and this is a recollection of those things which our soul once beheld, when it journeyed with God and, lifting its vision above the things which we now say exist, rose up into real being. And therefore it is just that the mind of the philosopher only has wings, for he is always, so far as he is able, in communion through memory with those things the communion with which causes God to be divine." [*Phaedrus* 249C]

Epilogue: The Holy Word

And beyond Indus and its tribute rivers . . .
And up the green ravine, across the vale,
Beside the windless and crystalline pool—

has made many think of the Cave of Amarnath. That, too, is a
goal of pilgrimages which enact, no doubt, as Prometheus's Cave
does, a beyond . . . .

The danger, as ever, is in literalism, idolatry. Prometheus and
his Oceanides are immortals and *either* eternal (and therefore
unimaginable) *or* mere perpetuals, everlastings, objects with an
unbounded durability (and therefore insipid). Homer himself
suffered pre-eminently from this difficulty. Not even the greatest
poets know what to do with unlimited free time. The Olympians
are almost extinguished with boredom: their only resources
are feasts, eroticism, and quarreling. As soon as Prometheus is
released Shelley faces this insoluble problem, and faces it frankly
and courageously.

He struggles with it for about twenty lines (III, 3, 22–39).
The moment this Cave has turned into

A simple dwelling, which shall be our own,

—an ideal perfectly fitted to harassed mortals—the question "What
on earth are immortals to do there?" is upon him. He tries a
remote, diluted echo or two from *King Lear* (V, 3, 8–20). But
Prometheus and his companions are not "birds i' the cage." In
immediate conjunction with "As the world ebbs and flows," the
fatal words "ourselves unchanged" are uttered. With all that we
know of his history around him, Lear can say

we'll wear out
In a wall'd prison, packs and sects of great ones
That ebb and flow by the moon

—but Prometheus's victory has cost him his qualification. And
his further efforts only lead into a shallower welter of triviality.
He recognizes this in the brave words "Our unexhausted spirits,"
but the game is up. Only one activity can truly kill time,
and that is Poetry itself and the other Arts—creative activity.

Beyond

Prometheus turns then to the exploration of the mystery of the service of imagination to man. That is what this Cave is for:

Such virtue has the cave and place around.

The exploration of imagination and its reference to reality does not necessarily, or ordinarily, lead to mysticism. With Shelley it did. His own experience of inspiration was decisive for him. His descriptions in prose and in verse make this very clear. *Defence of Poetry* is the most sustained of these affirmations and the best known. I will quote from only one sentence: "Poetry . . . expresses those arrangements of language . . . which are created by that imperial faculty, whose throne is curtained within the invisible nature of man." Those to whom the word *imperial* is evidence enough of depravity in its user may find Shelley's sense for it surprising. To explore the reach of this we may add, from his *Essay on Christianity:*

> Our most imperial and stupendous faculties—those on which the majesty and the power of humanity is erected—are, relatively to the inferior portion of its mechanism, active and imperial; but they are the passive slaves of some higher and more omnipotent Power.

And from the same:

> We live and move and think; but we are not the creators of our own origin and existence . . . we are not the masters of our own imaginations and moods of mental being. There is a Power by which we are surrounded, like the atmosphere in which some motionless lyre is suspended, which visits with its breath our silent chords at will.

The passage in Act III, scene 3, which has been under examination, moves, it will be noted, on from "Our unexhausted spirits" to the study of creation via the image of an Æolean Lute or Lyre. This may have come to him from Coleridge—from *The Æolean Harp* or *Dejection: an Ode*. In any case he made great use of it: in stanza 5 of the *Ode to the West Wind,* for example. Here it is the prelude to a wide survey of influences by which the creative mind can be touched. The passage (ll. 40–62)

Epilogue: The Holy Word

And hither come, sped on the charmèd winds,
Which meet from all the points of heaven, as bees
From every flower aëreal Enna feeds,
At their known island-homes in Himera,
The echoes of the human world, which tell
Of the low voice of love, almost unheard,
And dove-eyed pity's murmured pain, and music,
Itself the echo of the heart, and all
That tempers or improves man's life, now free;
And lovely apparitions,—dim at first,
Then radiant, as the mind, arising bright
From the embrace of beauty (whence the forms
Of which these are the phantoms) casts on them
The gathered rays which are reality—
Shall visit us, the progeny immortal
Of Painting, Sculpture, and rapt Poesy,
And arts, though unimagined, yet to be.
The wandering voices and the shadows these
Of all that man becomes, the mediators
Of that best worship love, by him and us
Given and returned; swift shapes and sounds, which grow
More fair and soft as man grows wise and kind,
And, veil by veil, evil and error fall:

is one of the most complex even in Shelley, and a gloss may be
helpful.

Upon the liberated mind converge the "echoes," or reflections,
of all its voices—the whisper of love, the murmur of pity, and
Music (itself doubly an echo)[8] and all that "tempers and
improves"; and come to us further, the ever-living offspring of
the other arts: Painting, Sculpture, inspired Poetry and unknown
arts of the future (the Cinema?). These offspring are epiphanies,
divine visitations, which grow brighter as (in the measure in
which) the mind—exalted and illumined from the "embrace" of
Intellectual Beauty (the Idea of the Good, the One, the Uncondi-

8. As Robert Bridges pointed out, this is from *Twelfth Night*, II, 4, 21:
"It gives a very echo to the seat where Love is thron'd" (*The Spirit of Man*,
Note to Fourth Impression).

tioned, the Indivisible, the Source Itself of the Forms, the Intelligible World, of which these messengers themselves are derived appearances)—reflects upon them the "gathered rays," the recollected, re-concentrated light which makes them what they are: the wandering voices and the shadows ("shadow of Beauty unbeheld") of "all that man becomes": of all that is fitting to him and of that greatness into which he will unfold; which voices (echoes) and shadows are the "mediators," in the theological sense, and the daemons (see *Symposium* 202E), as well as means, of "that best worship, love," reciprocal between Man and "us"; that is, that which, in the gathered rays, Prometheus and Asia would represent; these "swift" (fleeting? transient?) phantoms and echoes grow "more fair and soft" ("such strength is in meekness," II, 2, 94) as, in the measure in which, Man grows in wisdom and love, and evil and error, the veils of Reality, fall.

Such a gloss, of course, by no means catches all the meaning. We may remember, from *Defence:*

All high poetry is infinite; it is as the first acorn, which contained all oaks potentially. Veil after veil may be undrawn, and the inmost naked beauty of the meaning never exposed.

What it may bring out, however, is how true to the Plotinian tradition of mysticism Shelley is. *"Ex divina pulchritudine esse omnium derivatur"* ("From the divine Beauty the being of everything is derived"), to quote Dionysius the Areopagite from an apocryphal work attributed to Aquinas.

Another characteristic of Shelley's poetry is also remarkable here: its *involvedness.* I do not mean only that the syntax is involved—though it is amazingly so—or only that the thought and feeling themselves are so highly *introverted,* in the technical sense used in the discussion of mysticism; but that the meanings of these lines return within themselves. The lovely apparitions offered by the Arts become illumined when the mind casts on them, as a vast concave mirror might, the gathered rays; and yet it is such an apparition—Prometheus, namely—who is here speaking, and speaking, I suggest, knowingly as such. He is describing himself (and Asia, his *Shakti*) as "wandering voices" and "shadows" of "all that man becomes," as "mediators" able to be given "that best worship, love" by man and *to return it*. This "mind arising bright from the embrace of beauty" is no separate individual mind spellbound in adoration of its own products, though guided and saved by them. It is an ultimately inclusive whole achieving in this way its own self-realization.

Earth, who, in *Timaeus* 40C, is "the most venerable of the gods within the Heaven," is here a being of extraordinary authority, knowing the tongue that is

> Known
> But to the uncommunicating dead,

and able to tell Asia (III, 3, 113), from them, that

> Death is the veil which those who live call life:
> They sleep, and it is lifted.

She has been made mad (III, 3, 123) by Prometheus's pain, poisoned and poisonous by Jove's reign (I, 170–80; III, 3, 94). Henceforth she is to be, in Demogorgon's words (IV, 519),

> calm empire of a happy soul . . .
> . . . gathering as thou dost roll
> The love which paves thy path along the skies.

This Earth it is who directs Prometheus and Asia to "their destined cave." Caves have so great an importance in Shelley that it is worth noting how carefully this cave—on which Prometheus's thought at the moment of his release has dwelt so lovingly; after his salutations, it is the first thing he speaks of—is connected with Apollo's oracle on the rocky floor of Pytho (III, 3, 124–30) and, perhaps, with "the mighty portal" (II, 3, 2):

> Whence the oracular vapour is hurled up
> Which lonely men drink wandering in their youth.
> And call truth, virtue, love, genius, or joy,

and, perhaps, too, with (II, 2, 52):

> a plume-uplifting wind
> Which drives them on their path, while they
> Believe their own swift wings and feet
> The sweet desires within obey.

Evidence, to be weighed, that this most characteristic Shelleyan cave—like some of the others—is the throne room of Poetry itself, as he defines it in *Defence*, and that the fountain which

> Leaps in the midst with an awakening sound

is the very head and spring of inspiration.

Such, then, is the "Holy Word" *Prometheus Unbound* conveys. The phrase leads us, of course, to Blake:

> Hear the voice of the Bard!
> Who Present, Past, & Future, sees;
> Whose ears have heard
> The Holy Word
> That walk'd among the ancient trees,
>
> Calling the lapsed Soul,
> And weeping in the evening dew;
> That might controll
> The starry pole,
> And fallen, fallen light renew!

Songs of Experience, beginning so, end with:

> Youth of delight, come hither,
> And see the opening morn,
> Image of truth new born.
> Doubt is fled, & clouds of reason . . .

And here, to close, is Blake's vision of Eden (*Jerusalem* 38, 17–22):

> "We live as One Man; for contracting our infinite senses
> "We behold multitude, or expanding, we behold as one,
> "As One Man all the Universal Family, and that One Man

Epilogue: The Holy Word

"We call Jesus the Christ; and he in us and we in him
"Live in perfect harmony in Eden, the land of life,
"Giving, receiving, and forgiving each other's trespasses.

This last line, well understood, could be our Key to Paradise.